WHERE WE GO WHEN WE DIE

LIFE AFTER DEATH ACROSS THE UNIVERSE

MICHAEL VINCENT

HAVONA PRESS

CONTENTS

INTRODUCTION

There is a question we all carry but stop asking, convinced no answer exists. The question is simple: *Where do we go when we die?*

Not the biological mechanics—those you know. Cells cease functioning. Brain activity stops. The form remains; the life departs. This is observable, measurable, the realm of science and certainty.

But *you*. The awareness reading these words right now. The consciousness that has been continuous since you first recognized yourself as separate from the world around you. The *I* that has persisted through every change your body has undergone, every modification your mind has experienced, every moment from childhood to now. What happens to *that*?

You have been offered answers. Heaven and hell. Reincarnation. Oblivion. Energy returning to the cosmos. The ancestors. The void. Each tradition, each philosophy, each religion claims to know.

And yet none of them satisfy. Not really. Not when you are alone with unresolved questions, when someone you love is dying, or when you yourself face the abyss and discover that inherited beliefs ring offer little.

This book offers something different.

I am no wiser than those who came before. I have not personally traversed death and returned to map the territory. But I have encountered teachings so specific, so *detailed* in their description of what lies beyond mortality that they utterly transform this mystery.

BEYOND COMFORT

You do not need another book telling you to have faith or trust the universe. These phrases, however well-intentioned, are anesthesia—dulling the pain of uncertainty without addressing its source.

You need *information*. Actual description of what happens after the last breath. Geographic specificity about where consciousness goes. Mechanical detail about how survival works. The kind of knowledge that allows you to *prepare* rather than merely hope.

You will encounter concepts that challenge everything you thought you knew. You will be asked to expand your sense of what is possible far beyond anything your current worldview accommodates. You will discover that the universe is stranger yet more meticulously organized than you imagined.

What if death is really a portal we all go through? What if consciousness does not extinguish but reawakens? What if every person you have loved and lost is not *gone* but *somewhere*—actual places with names, with geography, with societies as real as any you have known?

What if the grief you carry is based on a fundamental misunderstanding of what death really is?

WHAT THIS BOOK CONTAINS

I will not tell you to believe. I will not ask you to have faith. I will not offer vague reassurances or empty promises.

I will *describe*, as specifically and concretely as discretion permits and language allows, what happens after death. Where consciousness awakens. What you will see, whom you will meet, and what you will do.

I will trace the path from mortal death through realms you cannot currently perceive, through training grounds designed for souls learning to function beyond flesh, through spheres of increasing magnificence, all the way to the center of reality itself.

I will explain *why*. Why suffering exists if the universe is benevolent. Why growth requires intelligent effort. Why you were made imperfect and why this is a gift rather than a curse.

And I will bring it back, always back, to *you*. To your daily life, your current choices, your present moment. Because cosmic truth that does not illuminate daily life is not truth worth having.

WHAT YOU RISK BY READING

You risk hope. The kind that, once kindled, cannot easily be extinguished. The kind that changes how you face mortality—your own and others'. The kind that makes sorrow bearable, not by diminishing it, but by providing context.

You risk transformation. Because you cannot see things differently without *being* different. You cannot grasp the architecture of eternity and remain unchanged. The person who finishes this book might not be quite the same as the person who began it.

You risk disappointment. If these teachings prove false, if death is indeed ending and survival illusion, then the hope I offer becomes cruelty. Better not to hope at all than to hope in vain—or so the logic goes.

> *To the unbelieving materialist, man is simply an evolutionary accident. His hopes of survival are strung on a figment of mortal imagination; his fears, loves, longings, and beliefs are but the reaction of the incidental juxtaposition of certain lifeless atoms of matter. No display of energy nor expression of trust can carry him beyond the grave.*

What if every intuition you've had about life beyond death was a glimpse of a deeper reality trying to break through? What if the people who told you death was the end were simply reporting the limits of their perception, mistaking the horizon for the edge of the world?

THE INVITATION

This book will not argue with you. It will not try to convince you through logic or rhetoric or emotional manipulation. It will simply *present*.

Read with skepticism. Read with rigor. But read with *openness*—the kind that can hold multiple possibilities simultaneously without collapsing into either blind faith or defensive dismissal.

You were not meant to live in terror of extinction. You were not designed to grieve without hope. You were not created to wonder whether your brief existence matters.

You were meant to *know*. Not with absolute certainty—that awaits direct experience—but with sufficient clarity to live courageously, to love deeply, to choose growth over stagnation because you understand what you are building and where it leads.

Begin Here

Turn the page. Take the first step on a path that leads somewhere extraordinary.

You may not believe everything you encounter here. You may resist, argue internally, dismiss parts as too strange or too specific or too good to be true.

That is fine, even expected.

But *continue*. Because scattered through what follows are seeds: ideas that will lodge in your consciousness, that will grow quietly, that will illuminate moments you have already lived and moments yet to come.

And perhaps you will discover what I discovered: that the universe is not silent on the question of death. That answers exist, detailed and specific and *verifiable through personal experience*. That hope is not delusion but recognition, a remembering of what some part of you has always known.

You are more than flesh. Death is not the end. Those you have lost are not lost. And the life you are living right now, this day, this choice, this moment, is material from which eternity is being built.

This is what the following pages will reveal. Not as a doctrine to accept, but as a map to explore.

The path is real. The destination exists. And you are already walking it, whether you know it or not.

Time to discover where it leads.

Turn the page.

1

—————

THE LAST BREATH AND THE FIRST AWAKENING

THERE IS A MOMENT EVERY HUMAN BEING FEARS—AND YET IT LEADS TO an awakening you will remember forever. You have been told lies about death: that it is the end of consciousness, or that it ushers you into some vague eternal state where you float in clouds singing endless hymns, or worse, that you will cease to exist, snuffed out like a candle flame.

None of this is true. What actually happens is far more sensible, far more beautiful, and far more aligned with everything you've always hoped might be real but were afraid to believe.

THE CROSSING

When the last breath leaves your body, there is a brief pause—not unconsciousness exactly, but a transition so smooth it resembles falling asleep in one room and waking in another.

You are not your body. You are a soul that has been forming and growing throughout your entire life. Every choice you made that aligned with truth, every moment you chose love over fear, courage over comfort, service over selfishness—all of this became part of your perpetual self. This is what survives.

1

But survival is not automatic. There must be something to survive: a soul with substance, a self that has become more than biological. For those who have lived with even a spark of faith, with even the smallest reaching upward, this threshold is crossed easily. The soul has formed. The identity persists.

Between death and reawakening, you do not experience the passage of time. Whether days or centuries pass on Earth, for you there is no waiting, no darkness, no lonely void.

> *The soul is wholly unconscious during the period from death to reper-sonalization and is in the keeping of the seraphic destiny guardian throughout this season of waiting.*[1]

One moment you are taking your last breath; the next, you are opening your eyes in a new world.

THE AWAKENING

You wake in what are called resurrection halls—immense, beautiful structures on the first mansion world, designed specifically to receive those who have graduated from mortality. Multitudes awaken here, each attended by celestial beings whose purpose is to welcome the newly arrived and ease the transition.

> *From the Temple of New Life there extend seven radial wings, the resurrection halls of the mortal races. There are one hundred thousand personal resurrection chambers in each of these seven wings. Throughout all eternity you will recall the profound memory impressions of your first witnessing of these resurrection mornings.*[2]

The first thing you notice is the light. It is everywhere, but it does not hurt your eyes. It seems to emanate from within things as much as from above them. The atmosphere has a quality you have never experienced—colors that have no names in human language, an air that feels alive with peace.

The second thing you notice is that you are you. Completely, unmistakably yourself. Not younger, not older, but somehow the truest version of yourself you have ever been. If you died aged and bent, you do not wake aged and bent. You wake as the person you always were beneath the accumulated effects of biology and time—the essential you, freed from the limitations of flesh.

> *The indwelling spirit is the eternal custodian of your ascending identity, the absolute assurance that you yourself and not another will occupy the form created for your personality awakening.*[3]

The third thing you notice is that you are not alone. Your seraphic guardian—the angel who has watched over you since childhood, who protected and guided you through mortal life in ways you never perceived—is present. She has carried your soul safely through the transition and now welcomes you to your new existence.

What Comes Next

The mansion worlds are not the destination. They are the beginning.

You are here to continue growing. The person you were on Earth was real but incomplete—a seed that has now sprouted, a child who must now learn to walk in larger worlds. On these training spheres, you will learn truths that were impossible to grasp while encased in flesh. You will come to understand the architecture of the cosmos, the purpose of your existence, the nature of the God who made you.

You will be reunited with others you have loved. Love is never lost here. Every genuine relationship endures, transfigured and purified of the misunderstandings and limitations that plagued it on Earth.

You will meet new companions from this and other worlds who are walking the same upward path. You will work, for meaningful service is one of the great joys of existence. You will learn, create, discover, and grow in ways you could not have imagined as a mortal.

And at the center of it all, you will begin to truly know the presence of God that has lived within you since you first became capable of moral choice—the divine gift that has been patiently guiding you your entire life, speaking in the silence, hoping you would turn inward and listen. Now, finally, that conversation can begin in earnest.

The Promise

Every person you have loved, who died with even the smallest amount of goodness, woke up. They opened their eyes in halls of resurrection surrounded by beings who welcomed them home. They began the next chapter of an adventure that never ends.

They are learning now. Growing now. Waiting for those they love to join them.

And when your time comes, when your last breath becomes your first awakening, you will find that everything you feared was a lie, and everything you hoped was true was only the faintest shadow of a reality more glorious than you could have imagined.

You wake up. You are greeted. You are loved. You are home in a way you never quite were on Earth.

And the journey—the real journey—has only just begun.

In the chapters that follow, we will walk together through this progression. We will explore each stage of the ascent, from the mansion worlds through realms beyond current comprehension, all the way to the center of all things. We will understand not just where you are going, but *why*—the purpose behind the design, the love that holds it all together.

But we begin here, with this single truth: You do not end. You continue. And what continues is beautiful beyond measure.

2

THE MANSION WORLDS

LEARN TO LIVE AGAIN

You are standing on a world. Not Earth, but a sphere that exists within the same cosmic neighborhood—part of a vast architecture of worlds designed as schools and homes for those ascending from mortality. This is the first of seven mansion worlds, each one a stage in your continuing development.

The resurrection halls overlook gardens of extraordinary beauty, and beyond them rise cities designed by beings who understand that beauty is not decoration but necessity, that architecture can evoke wonder. Everything here is real—more real, in fact, than anything you experienced on Earth. The ground beneath your feet has substance. The air carries scents that awaken something deep within you—not memories of places you have been, but recognition of what home truly means.

This world is not heaven in the ultimate sense. It is the first rung of a ladder that stretches upward through realms of increasing glory. But compared to Earth, it might as well be paradise. Disease does not exist here. Conflict as you knew it is absent. The confusion and chaos of mortal life have been left behind. You have entered a realm where growth is the purpose, service is the joy, and every soul is moving—at their own pace, by their own choices—toward perfection.

What moves you most is not the astonishing beauty of this new world, but what it represents: the care, the precision, the sheer *thoughtfulness* with which the universe has prepared for your continuation.

> *All fifty-six of the encircling worlds of the system capital are devoted to the transitional culture of ascending mortals, but the seven satellites of world number one are more specifically known as the mansion worlds.*[1]

Nothing about your survival is accidental. Nothing about what comes after death is vague or improvised. These worlds are as real as the chair you're sitting in now, as specific as the street address of your childhood home. They have topography, cities, ecosystems, and cultures. They have purpose.

And that purpose is you.

Waking to New Life

You have awakened on the first of these seven worlds, and already you are beginning to understand how profoundly you misunderstood the universe while you were mortal. Everything you thought was solid—matter, flesh, the ground beneath your feet—was only one narrow band of existence, like seeing only red in a spectrum that contains infinite colors.

Here, you can perceive more. Not everything—you are still so young in cosmic terms, still so new—but more. You can feel the energies that flow through all things. You can sense the substance of other beings in a way that transcends mere sight. When your seraphic guardian stands beside you, you don't just see her form; you sense her character, her kindness, and her nature in ways that would have been completely intangible to your mortal senses.

The first mansion world exists primarily for one purpose: to correct the *biological* and *environmental* deficiencies of your mortal life, those that prevented you from reaching your full potential on Earth.

Did you grow up in poverty, never having the chance to develop your mind? Here, you will learn. Were you stunted by illness, by disability, by circumstances beyond your control? Here, you will flourish. Did you die too young, before you could fully grasp what it meant to be alive? Here, you will be given all the time you need to become who you were always meant to be.

Your new form may surprise you. It is real, tangible, capable of sensation—yet fundamentally different from the flesh you left behind.

Morontia. This is the word for what you have become. Not quite material, not quite spiritual, but a blend of both, a form between. A form that is real, tangible, recognizable, but no longer subject to disease, decay, or death. A body of light and substance that can touch and be touched, that can feel joy more keenly than you ever felt it in the flesh.

Though you have morontia bodies, you continue through all seven of these worlds to eat, drink, and rest. You partake of the morontia order of food, a kingdom of living energy unknown on the material worlds. Both food and water are fully utilized in the morontia body; there is no residual waste.

You are still near human on this first world, not far removed from the limited viewpoints of mortal life, but each world discloses definite progress. From sphere to sphere you grow less material, more intellectual, and slightly more spiritual. The spiritual progress is greatest on the last three of these seven progressive worlds.[2]

YOUR FIRST DAYS

Upon awakening, you are not immediately thrust into curriculum. The transition from mortality to morontia life is given space to settle.

From the resurrection halls you proceed to the sector where you are assigned permanent residence. Then you enter upon ten days of personal liberty. You are free to explore the immediate vicinity of your new home and to familiarize yourself with the program which lies immediately ahead. You also have time to gratify your desire to consult the registry and call upon your loved ones and other earth friends who may have preceded you to these worlds.[3]

Ten days to wander, to explore, to find those you lost. Ten days to sit with the staggering reality that you survived death, that the universe prepared a place for you. Ten days before the structured work of ascension begins.

THE WORK OF PROGRESS

While life on these reconstruction worlds is refreshingly wonderful compared to earthly existence, it's not a vacation. These worlds are not clouds and harps and endless leisure. They are schools, and you are here to learn.

But what learning feels like when you are no longer tired, no longer distracted by pain or hunger or the static of a deteriorating body! Every lesson lands with crystalline clarity. Every insight builds on the last. You discover capacities in yourself you never knew existed.

You study the nature of the universe. Not dry facts, but living truth. You learn about energy and how it becomes matter and mind and spirit. You learn about personality and why you are eternally, irreplaceably *you*, no matter how much you change. You learn about the hierarchy of beings that fills the cosmos, from the lowest to the highest, and where you fit in that great chain of existence.

And you learn about God—not as a mere idea, but as a universal fact as well as a knowable person. Not all at once, but piece by piece, as your mind expands to contain larger and larger truths.

The Seven Mansion Worlds

The first world is for remedial work—not punishment, but repair. Making up what was lost, healing what was broken, building the foundation that mortality denied you.

> *You will resume your intellectual training and spiritual development at the exact level whereon they were interrupted by death. You begin over there right where you leave off down here.*[4]

The second mansion world is where you truly begin to function as a cosmic citizen. Here, the confusion of mortal life—the mental disorders, the chemical imbalances, the conflicts that made you your own worst enemy—all of this is resolved.

And everything worth keeping from your mortal mind—every meaningful memory, every hard-won insight—has been preserved. What was animalistic and purely material perished with the brain. But everything of survival value remains, counterparted by the divine spirit, retained as part of your personal memory throughout the entire ascendant career.

You emerge from the second world stable, sound, ready to move forward without the internal sabotage that made mortal life so exhausting.

On the third mansion world, you experience true personal culture for the first time. All the beauty that human civilization managed to create—the art, the music, the philosophy, the aspiration toward new heights—this was only a pale echo of what is possible here. You learn to create in ways that would seem like magic to your mortal self. Social life is beautifully enhanced, as people who are learning to be honest, kind, and sincerely interested in one another live and work together.

The fourth mansion world is where you truly begin to understand your place in the larger cosmos. You are not just an individual; you are part of an extensive enterprise far beyond your personal concerns.

You begin to grasp the social and spiritual realities that bind all beings together, from the lowest to the highest. You learn citizenship, not just of a world or a nation, but of a universe.

> *A new social order is being introduced, one based on the under-standing sympathy of mutual appreciation, the unselfish love of mutual service, and the overmastering motivation of the realization of a common and supreme destiny—the Paradise goal of worshipful and divine perfection.*[5]

On the fifth mansion world, you learn the language spoken throughout the local universe, a means of communication that can convey truth with precision and beauty. More than this, you begin to truly appreciate the journey that lies ahead of you. You can see, dimly at first but then with growing clarity, the path that stretches from where you are to heights you can barely imagine—the spheres you will traverse, the beings you will become.

> *A real birth of cosmic consciousness takes place on this world. Study is becoming voluntary, unselfish service natural, and worship sponta-neous. A real morontia character is budding; a real morontia creature is evolving.*[6]

> *The shadow of the mortal nature grows less and less as these worlds are ascended one by one. You are becoming more and more adorable as you leave behind the coarse vestiges of planetary animal origin. "Coming up through great tribulation" serves to make glorified mortals very kind and understanding, very sympathetic and tolerant.*[7]

The sixth mansion world is where your will and divine will start to align so naturally that you can hardly distinguish between them. You begin to understand that the purpose of your existence is not merely to survive, not merely to be happy, but to become an instrument through which divinity can experience life from your unique perspective.

And on the seventh mansion world, you are prepared for graduation. You are freed from the last remnants of your mortal limitations. You are almost ready to leave these training worlds behind and begin the next stage of your ascent.

*fusion, and by the time you have finished, you will be full-fledged
morontians.*[9]

Time Without Pressure

How long does all this take? There are no calendars here counting
down the days. You have all the time that exists, all the time you need.

Some pass through the mansion worlds quickly, their souls already
well-formed. Others take longer. The universe is patient. God is
patient. Your teachers are patient. And you learn patience too—not
the grim endurance of waiting for suffering to end, but the peaceful
confidence that comes from knowing that everything needful will be
accomplished in its proper time.

You might spend more time on a single concept, wrestling with it,
turning it over in your mind, discussing it with companions, bringing
it to your teachers, until finally, it clicks, and you understand. And in
that moment of understanding, you grow. Your soul expands. Your
capacity increases. You become more than you were. And then you
move on to the next lesson, the next challenge, the next beautiful
truth waiting to be discovered.

Not Alone

One of the great revelations of the mansion worlds is this: you are
not, and never will be, alone.

The loved ones you grieved—they are here, somewhere in these
worlds or beyond them, continuing their own paths. You will see
them—not constantly (everyone has their own work to do)—but regu-
larly, joyfully. The bonds formed in mortality do not break; they
strengthen, purified of all the petty conflicts and misunderstandings
that plagued them when you were both confined to flesh.

But more than this, you make new friends. Companions who died in
other times or on other worlds, who are walking the same path you
are walking. You discover that personality is universal—that beings

from distant worlds can become as dear to you as anyone you knew on Earth, because authentic connection transcends all incidents of origin.

THE LIFE YOU LIVE

What does a day look like on the mansion worlds? If you can call it a day—the light here does not come from a sun that rises and sets, but from a more constant, pervasive source.

You wake, you sleep, though it is refreshing in a way mortal sleep never was. You live in a beautiful, simple dwelling suited to your needs, a space that is *yours*, a place of rest and contemplation. You eat, and the foods here nourish you in ways both subtle and sustaining.

You work. Perhaps you are assigned to help newly arrived survivors adjust to their new existence. Perhaps you work in one of the breathtaking gardens that beautify these worlds. Perhaps you labor in some creative or administrative capacity, contributing to the smooth functioning of mansion world society. The work is meaningful, and you feel that meaning in every task.

You study. Hours spent in libraries that would make Alexandria weep with envy, or in classrooms where teachers who have lived for millennia share wisdom with students hungry to understand. You wrestle with concepts that would have been incomprehensible to your mortal mind, and slowly you master them.

You socialize. Conversations that range from light banter to profound philosophical discussion. Friendships that deepen over shared experiences. The discovery that you are truly interested in other people's stories, their perspectives—and that they are interested in yours.

You worship. Not out of obligation, but out of pure awe and gratitude. When you begin to truly understand what has been done for you—the patience, the provision, the sheer love that holds all of this together— worship becomes as natural as breathing. You find yourself spontaneously grateful, spontaneously reaching upward toward the Source of all this goodness.

You rest, and rest itself is holy. Time spent in quiet contemplation, in communion with the divinity within, in simple appreciation of endless beauty.

The Direction of All Things

Every lesson learned, every insight gained, every relationship deepened—all of it points in a single direction. Upward and inward. Toward perfection and toward Paradise.

You are not being prepared for an eternity of stasis, a frozen existence where nothing ever changes. You are being prepared for never-ending growth, service, and creative contribution to a universe that is itself still evolving toward some ultimate sublimity that even the highest beings cannot yet fully grasp.

The mansion worlds are the beginning, not the end. They are the place where you shed the last remnants of mortality, where you learn the fundamental truths that will serve you throughout all the ages to come.

And when you are ready, when you have learned all that these worlds have to teach, you will graduate. You will move on to worlds stranger and more wonderful than you can conceive.

But that is still ahead. For now, you are here. You are home. You are learning, growing, becoming. And that is exactly where you need to be.

3

REUNION

LOVE BEYOND DEATH

THE QUESTION THAT HAUNTS THE GRIEVING MORE THAN ANY OTHER IS this: *Will I see them again?*

Not in some vague, ethereal sense. Not as a disembodied spirit or a faded memory. But *them*—the actual person you loved, with their particular way of laughing, their specific quirks, their irreplaceable self. Will you embrace them again? Will you talk with them? Will they know you, and will you know them?

The answer is yes.

Those you loved who died before you—they are here. Not lost. Not dissolved into some impersonal cosmic energy. Not transformed beyond recognition. They are themselves, only more so—healed of whatever broke them in mortal life, freed from whatever bound them, radiant with a peace you always wished for them.

They have been waiting for you.

The reunion that follows cannot be adequately described in words, for it belongs to the realm of pure emotion, pure vindication, pure love proven stronger than death. All the years of separation collapse into nothing. All the grief you carried falls away. All the prayers you prayed—even the ones you were too hurt to voice—are suddenly, gloriously answered.

You see them again. You embrace them again. You continue with them a relationship that death interrupted but could not end.

RECOGNITION

When you awaken on the mansion worlds and see that loved one waiting for you, there is no confusion, no uncertainty. You know them instantly, not just by appearance, though the morontia form bears a clear resemblance to what they were. But by something deeper. You recognize their *essence*, the fundamental character that made them who they were.

This recognition goes both ways. They know you. Even though you are now in a form you've never worn before, even though you may look different in ways you can't quite articulate, they see *you*. The real you. The you that was always there beneath the aging flesh and accumulated scars of mortal life.

How is this possible? Because personality is immutable. It is...

> *the one changeless reality in an otherwise ever-changing creature experience; and it unifies all other associated factors of individuality. The personality is the unique bestowal which the Universal Father makes upon the living and associated energies of matter, mind, and spirit, and which survives with the survival of the soul.*[1]

It is the one thing about you that never changes, even as everything else does. The pattern that makes you uniquely yourself remains constant. And those who truly loved you learned to recognize that pattern, whether they knew it or not. They loved the real you, not just the temporary housing. And so they know you still.

Relationships Transformed

Love does not end at death. This is one of the great truths that mortals sense but rarely have confirmed: true love is eternal. The relationships you valued on Earth continue, but they also *improve*. All the petty irritations, the misunderstandings born of tired minds and strained circumstances, the friction that came from two imperfect beings trying to connect through human consciousness—all of this is gone.

What remains is the essence of what you were to each other. The genuine affection. The shared experiences. The ways you helped each other grow, whether you realized it at the time or not.

If you were married, that relationship continues—though it transcends the biological imperatives and social conventions that partly defined it on Earth. The deep partnership, the intimacy of truly knowing another soul, this not only survives but deepens.

If you were parent and child, that bond remains. The child who died young wakes as a child, and you will raise them on these worlds as you could not on Earth. The potential that was cut short is being fulfilled here. The child you raised to adulthood? You will watch them grow into cosmic citizens, share experiences that make your mortal time together seem like the first chapter of an infinitely long book. Either way, you understand: their death was not the end of their story. It was never the end.

If you were friends, siblings, companions of any kind—the love remains. Every relationship you formed on Earth becomes part of your endless existence. You do not lose people here. You *find* them, over and over, at different stages of the ascent.

On Earth, you likely hid parts of yourself from everyone, even those you loved most. You wore masks, played roles, presented carefully curated versions of yourself because you feared rejection, feared judgment, feared being truly seen.

Here, the masks fall away. Not all at once (even morontia mortals need time to learn vulnerability), but gradually, inevitably. You discover that you can be fully yourself—flaws and strengths, fears and hopes, the entire complicated truth of who you are—and you will not be rejected.

This transforms every relationship. Friendships deepen into profound understanding. Even casual acquaintances become meaningful, because you learn to see each other as you truly are, not as you pretend to be.

And strangers—beings you've never met before, who come from worlds you've never heard of, who have histories completely unlike your own—these can become friends as dear as anyone you knew on Earth. Because personality transcends all limitations of origin. A good soul is recognizable, whether it was born on Earth or elsewhere.

The Community of Ascenders

You are not making this voyage alone. All around you, at every stage, are fellow travelers who may have been born on different planets, who awakened on different mansion worlds, but who are all climbing the same cosmic ladder.

Some of these become friends. Deep, enduring friendships formed through shared experience, through helping each other master difficult lessons, through being loyal companions on a long journey together.

You learn from each other. Their insights illuminate your blind spots. Your strengths support their weaknesses. Together, you become more than you could have been separately.

You can be honest—fully, vulnerably honest—because everyone here is also learning, also struggling, also imperfect but striving. There is no judgment, only support. No competition, only collaboration. No zero-sum game where your gain is another's loss, but sincere joy in each other's progress.

The higher you ascend, the more lonely you become when temporarily without the association of your fellows.[2]

This is not a flaw in the design. It is evidence that your capacity for connection has grown. Shallow relationships can be interrupted without much pain. Deep ones cannot. The ache of temporary separation is the price of genuine belonging.

You realize: you will forever belong to a community of beings who understand you, support you, and ascend alongside you. The loneliness you sometimes felt in mortal life—the sense that no one truly understood you, that you were fundamentally alone in your experience—this dissolves in the company of fellow ascenders.

You were never meant to climb alone. And you never will.

What Love Becomes

From the vantage point of the mansion worlds, you begin to understand what you could not have seen while mortal: your earthly relationships were not the totality of what you could experience. They were the *beginning*.

The person you married and loved for fifty years? You will know them for fifty thousand years, fifty million, for all of eternity. And the love, expanded beyond human betrothal, will deepen with every age. The friend who understood you when no one else did? That understanding will expand as you both grow, until you know each other with depth and clarity.

Love, you discover, is not a finite resource that gets used up. It grows, expands, and becomes richer with every passing age. The universe is designed to support and deepen all connections.

4

THE SYSTEM HEADQUARTERS

COSMIC CITIZENSHIP

YOU HAVE COMPLETED THE MANSION WORLDS. SEVEN SPHERES OF transformation, seven awakenings, seven stages of becoming something more than you were. The last remnants of your animal origin have been purged. The final tendencies of unfortunate heredity and unwholesome environment have been eradicated. You are no longer merely a surviving mortal—you are ready to become a citizen.

And now, for the first time since you died, you will not need to sleep through your transition to the next world.

> *Seven times do those mortals who pass through the entire mansonia career experience the adjustment sleep and the resurrection awakening. But the last resurrection hall, the final awakening chamber, was left behind on the seventh mansion world. No more will a form-change necessitate the lapse of consciousness or a break in the continuity of personal memory.*[1]

You step onto Jerusem awake, aware, continuous. The you who arrives is the same you who departed, with no gap in consciousness, no break in the chain of identity. From this point forward, your

20

journey will be unbroken. You will never again lose yourself in the sleep of transformation.

A World Beyond Imagination

Jerusem is the capital of your local system—the administrative center for the six hundred and nineteen inhabited worlds of your local system, including your native Earth. It is almost one hundred times the size of your home planet, yet its gravity is slightly less. You feel lighter here, in every sense.

This is not a world that evolved. It was created—architected with intention, designed for purpose. There are no rugged mountain ranges born of tectonic violence, no scars of geological upheaval. Instead, there are beauteous highlands and unique variations of landscape that no evolutionary world could produce. Thousands upon thousands of small lakes sparkle across its surface, connected by gentle waterways. No raging rivers, no violent storms, no seasons of harsh cold or brutal heat. The temperature remains mild and constant, the light soft and even, emanating not from a single sun but sifting gently from all directions like perpetual morning.

> *Jerusem is indeed a foretaste of paradisiacal glory and grandeur. But you can never hope to gain an adequate idea of these glorious architectural worlds by any attempted description. There is so little that can be compared with aught on your world, and even then the things of Jerusem so transcend the things of Earth that the comparison is almost grotesque.*[2]

Jerusem teems with life—not just ascending mortals like yourself, but angels, administrators, Material Sons and Daughters, and beings of orders you have never encountered and can barely comprehend. This world exhibits all three phases of existence simultaneously: the material, the morontial, and the spiritual. Whether you are still largely material in nature, or have progressed to higher morontia states, or are visiting as a spirit being—you will feel at home here. Jerusem was designed to accommodate all.

The Architecture of Jerusem

Considerable portions of Jerusem are assigned as residential areas, while other portions of the system capital are given over to the necessary administrative functions involving the supervision of the affairs of 619 inhabited spheres, 56 transitional-culture worlds, and the system capital itself.[3]

The city is organized by geometric zones: circles for residential areas, squares for system-wide administration, rectangles where native beings gather, and triangles for local governance. This pattern repeats across every system capital in the local universe—a design chosen by the Creator Son himself.

This arrangement of the system activities into circles, squares, rectangles, and triangles is common to all the system capitals. In another universe an entirely different arrangement might prevail. These are matters determined by the diverse plans of the Creator Sons.[4]

The circles—seven concentric, successively elevated rings—house the residential areas of the celestial orders.

These circles are constructed of crystal gems of gleaming brightness, each outer ring overlooking the inner ones from elevated promenades. The gates that penetrate each wall—from fifty to one hundred and fifty thousand of them—consist of single pearly crystals. You can walk these promenades and observe beings you once only read about: Life Carriers, Melchizedeks, angels of every order. On the transitional-culture worlds, ascending mortals freely mingle with all orders of divine sonship.

The courtesy colonies—where diverse groups of celestial beings and ascending mortals reside temporarily—are graced by three enormous structures: a huge astronomic observatory, a gigantic art gallery, and an immense assembly hall devoted to rest and recreation.

Surrounding these circles is the exhibit panorama—five thousand standard miles (approximately 35,000 Earth miles) in circumference, presenting the advancing status of every inhabited world in the system, constantly revised to reflect current conditions on each planet.

I doubt not that this vast promenade will be the first sight of Jerusem to claim your attention when you are permitted extended leisure on your earlier visits.[5]

THE SEVEN TRANSITIONAL WORLDS

Orbiting Jerusem are seven enormous satellites, each about ten times the size of Earth. These are the transitional culture spheres—worlds dedicated to specific aspects of your continuing education. And orbiting each of these seven worlds are seven smaller spheres, making forty-nine subsatellites in all. The seven mansion worlds where you spent your initial afterlife training orbit the first of these transitional worlds.

You now have access to all of them.

The first transitional world is the Finaliter World—headquarters of those remarkable beings who have completed the entire Paradise journey and returned to serve. Throughout your mansion world experience, you made pilgrimages here, glimpsing these perfected beings when the energy transformers enabled you to perceive them. They seemed almost incomprehensible then—spirits of such attainment that they existed beyond your morontia vision. But they stood as living proof of what you would become. They had walked the path you were beginning. They had been mortal once, on worlds like yours.

Now, as a Jerusem citizen, you understand them better. You begin to grasp that the distance between what you are and what they have become, while intimidating, is traversable. Step by step, world by world, you will close that gap. The finaliters are not gods. They are graduates. And their presence here, serving beings so far below their station, speaks to the nature of perfection itself: glory bends to lift.

The other transitional worlds house different orders of beings and different functions. The Morontia World is where the supervisors of morontia life train their associates.

> *In passing through the seven mansion worlds, you will also progress through these cultural and social spheres of increasing morontia contact. When you advance from the first to the second mansion world, you will become eligible for a visitor's permit to transitional headquarters number two, the morontia world, and so on. And when present on any one of these six cultural spheres, you may, on invitation, become a visitor and observer on any of the seven surrounding worlds of associated group activities.*[6]

The Angelic World is the headquarters of all the seraphic hosts engaged in system activities and is surrounded by the seven worlds of angelic training and instruction. These are the seraphic social spheres. The World of the Sons is where divine Sons of various orders maintain their headquarters. The World of the Spirit acts as the rendezvous for high personalities of the Infinite Spirit. And the World of the Father is a silent sphere, containing a great temple of light at its center, open to all as worshipers, though no beings are domiciled there.

The World of the Father is surrounded by satellites that serve as detention spheres—the prison worlds where Lucifer and his followers remain confined, awaiting final judgment. As a seventh-mansion-world graduate, you are permitted to visit these isolation worlds. You can observe the archrebels themselves, those high beings who chose to reject the path you have embraced. It is a solemn sight, a warning written in living tragedy: even the most exalted can fall, and falling, they lose everything that made existence worthwhile.

THE MATERIAL SONS AND DAUGHTERS

The great divisions of celestial life have their headquarters and immense preserves on Jerusem, including the various orders of divine Sons, high spirits, superangels, angels, and midway creatures. The central abode of this wonderful sector is the chief temple of the Material Sons.[7]

Among the most fascinating residents of Jerusem are the Material Sons and Daughters—the Adams and Eves. These are not the specific Adam and Eve who came to your world and partially failed. These are an entire order of beings, created to serve as biological uplifters on evolutionary worlds, but residing in vast estates on system headquarters between assignments.

The domain of the Adams is the center of attraction to all new arrivals on Jerusem. It is an enormous area consisting of one thousand centers, although each family of Material Sons and Daughters lives on an estate of its own up to the time of the departure of its members for service on the evolutionary worlds of space or until their embarkation upon the Paradise-ascension career.[8]

They are the highest type of sex-reproducing beings in the training spheres of the universes. They are truly material—visible even to mortal eyes on the inhabited worlds—yet through the life currents of the system and the fruit of the Edentia shrub, they can live on indefinitely. They are the physical link between divinity above and humanity below, beings you can see and touch, who nonetheless possess natures far beyond your own.

You will spend much time among them.

No surviving mortal, midwayer, or seraphim may ascend to Paradise, attain the Father, and be mustered into the Corps of the Finality without having passed through that sublime experience of achieving parental relationship to an evolving child of the worlds or some other experience analogous and equivalent thereto. The relationship of child and parent is fundamental to the essential concept of the Universal Father and his universe children. Therefore does such an experience become indispensable to the experiential training of all ascenders.[9]

If you experienced parenthood during your mortal life—if you raised children, nurtured them, guided them, loved them through difficulty and celebrated their growth—then you carry that essential experience with you. But if you did not, if death came too soon or circumstances prevented it, then you will gain that experience here, in the homes of the Jerusem Adams and Eves, helping to raise their children, learning through direct participation what it means to be a parent.

There is also the probation nursery—a place on the Finaliter World where children who died before developing spiritual status are reassembled and raised. If you lost a child to early death, that child is here, growing, waiting. You may transfer to the nursery to raise them —reuniting with your own while fulfilling the parental experience requirement if you lacked it.

The Material Sons and Daughters become, in effect, your sponsors and mentors. They certify your readiness to leave Jerusem for the constellation worlds. No ascending mortal departs without their approval—without their confirmation that you have achieved a unified personality that blends your completed mortal experience with your budding morontia nature, all under the spiritual guidance of your indwelling spirit.

SCHOOLS OF SELF-GOVERNMENT

Jerusem is also a place of political education—though "political" may be too small a word for what you learn here.

The Melchizedeks, those versatile Sons who have guided ascending mortals since the first mansion world, conduct more than thirty educational centers here. These schools begin with the college of self-evaluation, where you learn to accurately assess yourself, and culminate in the schools of Jerusem citizenship, where you learn to participate in representative government at cosmic scale.

> *The entire universe is organized and administered on the representative plan. Representative government is the divine ideal of self-government among nonperfect beings.* [10]

You learn that every hundred years, your system elects ten representatives to sit in the constellation legislature. These representatives are chosen by the Jerusem council of one thousand electors—all of whom are graduates of the highest Melchizedek school of administration. Suffrage is universal among the three citizenship groups: Material Sons and Daughters, angels and their associates, and ascending mortals like yourself. But votes are weighted by wisdom—specifically, by your demonstrated attainment of morontia insight. Your vote can be worth anywhere from one to one thousand, depending on your certified progress.

This is not democracy as you knew it on Earth. This is something more nuanced: a system where everyone participates, but where wisdom counts more heavily than mere opinion. You are being trained for citizenship not just in a local system, but in a universe where beings of very different natures and capacities must coordinate their efforts toward common goals.

THE SEA OF GLASS

Near Jerusem's polar region lies the sea of glass—an enormous circular crystal, one hundred miles in circumference and thirty miles deep. This is where transport seraphim arrive and depart, where the broadcasts from across the universe are received.

> *Of all preoccupations for an ascendant mortal on Jerusem, none is more engaging and engrossing than that of listening in on the never-ending stream of universe space reports.* [11]

From the sea of glass, you can hear messages from Salvington, the capital of your local universe. You receive regular word from Edentia, the constellation headquarters, where the Most High Constellation Fathers rule. Periodically, you hear broadcasts relayed from Uversa, capital of the superuniverse. And when messages come from Paradise itself—from the very center of all things—the entire population gathers, and the broadcasts become visible through techniques of reflectivity that project the content across the crystalline expanse.

You begin to grasp, in a new way, how expansive the universe really is —and how connected. Events on worlds you have never visited affect beings you have never met. Decisions made at the highest levels ripple down through local universes, constellations, systems, and individual planets. You are part of something far larger than you imagined, and that something communicates, coordinates, and ensures nothing or no one is lost.

CITIZENSHIP

When you have completed your training on Jerusem—when you have learned what the Melchizedeks teach, when you have gained parental experience among the Material Sons and Daughters, when you have demonstrated the unified personality that qualifies you to advance— you will be certified as ready to leave.

You will not be the same being who arrived from the seventh mansion world. You have become a citizen of the system. You understand now how complex organizations function without chaos. You know how billions of beings coordinate their efforts toward common purposes. You have begun to grasp the representative government by which the universe administers itself. You have glimpsed, in the finaliters, what completion looks like—and you have accepted that you are walking the same path.

What is daily life like here?

> *The activities of such a world are of three distinct varieties: work, progress, and play. Stated otherwise, they are: service, study, and relaxation. The composite activities consist of social intercourse, group entertainment, and divine worship.*[12]

You are not just passing through. You are living here—fully, joyfully, usefully.

The constellation training worlds await. Seventy spheres of even higher culture, where you will learn group ethics at cosmic scales. You are ready.

But before you go, pause. Look back at the mansion worlds, at your first stumbling steps into the afterlife. Look at how far you have come. And then look forward, at the path still ahead—the constellation, the local universe capital, the superuniverse, Havona, and Paradise itself.

You are climbing. Step by step, sphere by sphere, you are becoming what you were always meant to be. And Jerusem—this first true citizenship, this first participation in the representative government of the universe—is where you learned that you belong to a coordinated whole, a republic of worlds.

You belong to it. And it belongs to you.

5

THE CONSTELLATION WORLDS

THE GARDENS OF GOD

You have been a student. You have been a citizen. Now you enter the most settled period of your entire morontia career—seventy worlds of training where you learn to live joyfully with beings like and unlike yourself.

Your constellation awaits. Seven hundred seventy-one architectural spheres encircling Edentia, an enormous capital world. Here you will achieve something that was impossible while you still carried the remnants of animal nature: true socialization of your evolving personality.

> *This entire sojourn on the constellation training worlds, culminating in Edentia citizenship, is a period of true and heavenly bliss.*[1]

You are entering a phase of existence where struggle gives way to stability, where the constant transformation of earlier stages settles into steady growth. You will still change, still learn, still become more than you are. But the jarring adjustments are behind you. From here, you progress as yourself—a self that has finally become unified enough to simply be while simultaneously becoming.

The Gardens of God

Edentia is beautiful beyond your capacity to imagine. The system capital Jerusem was glorious, but Edentia surpasses it. While universe headquarters worlds reflect spiritual grandeur, and system capitals showcase material and mineral construction, the constellation capitals are the acme of living embellishment.

> *About one half of Edentia is devoted to the exquisite gardens of the Most Highs, and these gardens are among the most entrancing morontia creations of the local universe. This explains why the extraordinarily beautiful places on the inhabited worlds are so often called "the garden of Eden."*[2]

When you walked through the most beautiful natural places on Earth —gardens that took your breath away, landscapes that brought tears to your eyes—you were glimpsing, however faintly, what the celestial artisans achieve on Edentia as a matter of course. Here, living materials are used instead of inert paint and lifeless marble. Botanic artistry reaches levels that would have seemed impossible to your mortal mind. The unique creatures who serve as the landscape architects of the headquarters worlds work under the direction of the celestial artisans and the permanent citizens, creating environments of staggering beauty.

> *If you enjoy the flowers, shrubs, and trees of Earth, then will you feast your eyes upon the botanical beauty and the floral grandeur of these supernal gardens. But it is beyond my powers of description to undertake to convey to the mortal mind an adequate concept of these beauties of the heavenly worlds. Truly, eye has not seen such glories as await your arrival on these worlds of the mortal-ascension adventure.*[3]

The vegetation here is unlike anything you knew in mortal life. There are material growths with characteristic green coloration, yes—but there are also morontia plants, energy growths with violet and orchid hues that vary and reflect in ways your eyes could never have perceived before. When eaten, these morontia plants leave no residual waste; they are pure energy, nourishment fully absorbed.

And the animals—thousands upon thousands of beautiful living creatures. No carnivores, no predators, no struggle for survival. Nothing here wants to harm anything else. Nothing competes for resources. The "survival of the fittest" that characterized your evolutionary world has been replaced by creative adaptation that foreshadows the perfection of the eternal worlds.

Even the distinctively animal life is very different from that of the evolutionary worlds, so different that it is quite impossible to portray to mortal minds the unique character and affectionate nature of these nonspeaking creatures. The whole animal creation is of an entirely different order from the gross animal species of the evolutionary planets. But all this animal life is most intelligent and exquisitely serviceable, and all the various species are surprisingly gentle and touchingly companionable. There is nothing in all Edentia to make any living being afraid.[4]

The Permanent Citizens

You will not be alone on Edentia. Besides your fellow ascending mortals, besides the administrators and teachers, you will live among the univitatia—the permanent citizens of the constellation worlds.

These children of the Creator Son and Creative Spirit exist on a plane between material and spiritual. They are not morontia creatures like yourself, but something else entirely. They inhabit all the worlds surrounding Edentia. Across the seventy major spheres, they exist in seventy orders—each with a different visible form.

As you progress through the constellation training worlds, your own morontia form will be attuned to correspond with the univitatia of each sphere. You will be rekeyed—adjusted, modified—each time you move from one major world to another. But unlike your earlier transitions, these changes will not require temporary loss of consciousness.

These permanent citizens are your training partners. Living with them, working with them, learning to understand beings so different from yourself—this is the heart of your constellation education.

> *Spiritually, the univitatia are alike; intellectually, they vary as do mortals; in form, they much resemble the morontia state of existence, and they are created to function in seventy diverse orders of personality.*[5]

Each order exhibits ten major variations of intellectual activity. Each variation presides over special training schools on one of the satellites orbiting the major worlds. The constellation training system contains seven hundred worlds of technical and practical education, open to all classes of intelligent beings.

THE SECRET OF JOYFUL RELATIONSHIP

What exactly will you learn on the seventy training worlds?

> *Your sojourn on Edentia and its associated spheres will be chiefly occupied with the mastery of group ethics, the secret of pleasant and profitable interrelationship between the various universe and superuniverse orders of intelligent personalities.*[6]

Group ethics. The secret of pleasant and profitable interrelationship. These phrases may sound academic, but they point to something deeply practical: how to live happily with others who are different from you.

On the mansion worlds, you unified your own personality—integrated the fragmented, conflicting aspects of yourself into a coherent whole. On Jerusem, you learned citizenship, how to participate in systems larger than yourself. But on Edentia, you tackle something even more challenging: genuine socialization with beings who think differently, perceive differently, exist differently than you do.

You will achieve simultaneous adjustment to both fellow ascenders and your hosts—learning to work effectively with your own order of beings while in close association with a very different order.

You will attain intellectual harmony and vocational adjustment with both groups of associates while furthering the progressive coordination of your Paradise ascension career.

And through all of this, you will develop something precious: the ability to live in intimate contact with beings both like and unlike yourself with ever-lessening irritability and ever-diminishing resentment.

This last phrase deserves attention. Ever-lessening irritability. Ever-diminishing resentment. The universe recognizes that these are not easy achievements. You will not arrive on Edentia already free of frustration with others. You will grow into that freedom, deliberately, over time, through practice.

> *Intellectually, socially, and spiritually two moral creatures do not merely double their personal potentials of universe achievement by partnership technique; they more nearly quadruple their attainment and accomplishment possibilities.*[7]

Partnership multiplies your potential. Collaboration does not merely add—it multiplies. But to access that multiplication, you must learn to work with very different beings. You must master the group ethics that make such partnership joyful rather than grinding.

The training is carefully sequenced. At first, you are outnumbered— one ascending mortal living among many permanent citizens, immersed in their reality, required to adapt while maintaining your own identity. Gradually, the ratio shifts. More of your fellow ascenders join you at each stage until, on the final worlds, you work as true partners—equal numbers, genuine collaboration between orders.

As you learn to socialize with beings unlike yourself, you simultaneously improve your relations with your fellow progressors. The skills transfer. The patience you develop with different beings makes you more patient with similar beings. The communication techniques you master across the gulf of otherness make you more articulate with those who share your background.

THE MOST HIGH FATHERS

The constellation is governed by the Most Highs—divine Sons of the local universe, beings of highest administrative wisdom whose jurisdiction spans one hundred systems, up to one hundred thousand inhabited worlds. Three of them serve together: the Constellation Father, who presides; the senior Most High; and the junior Most High. They rotate through these positions over periods of about fifty thousand years.

You may have encountered references to the Most Highs even in your mortal life. The Psalmist knew that Edentia was ruled by three Constellation Fathers when he wrote of "the tabernacles of the Most Highs." Daniel understood their function when he declared, "The Most High rules in the kingdom of men and gives it to whomsoever he will."

> *The Constellation Fathers are little occupied with the individuals of an inhabited planet, but they are closely associated with those legislative and lawmaking functions of the constellations which so greatly concern every mortal race and national group of the inhabited worlds.*[8]

The Most Highs govern not individual hearts but the affairs of nations. They shape the large-scale conditions under which mortal races develop. On normal worlds, their influence is indirect, exercised through the System Sovereign. But on isolated worlds like Earth—quarantined because of the Lucifer rebellion—the Most Highs exercise more direct oversight. They have maintained special supervision over your planet since Lucifer's fall, and they supervised all affairs concerning the Paradise bestowal when the Creator Son lived among you.

MOUNT ASSEMBLY AND THE FAITHFUL OF DAYS

On Edentia stands a most holy mount—the dwelling place of the Faithful of Days, a Son of the Paradise Trinity who serves as the personal representative of the Trinity in your constellation. This divine Son has been present since Edentia's creation, standing at the right hand of the Constellation Fathers, offering counsel when asked but never interfering unbidden.

On this consecrated highland the ascending mortals periodically assemble to hear this Son of Paradise tell of the long and intriguing journey of progressing mortals through the one billion perfection worlds of Havona and on to the indescribable delights of Paradise.[9]

Here, for the first time, you hear detailed descriptions of what lies ahead. The Faithful of Days speaks of Havona—one billion worlds of perfection circling the eternal center. He describes the journey through those worlds, the challenges and glories that await. He speaks of Paradise itself, the motionless Isle at the heart of all things, where the Trinity dwells.

These are no longer distant possibilities. They are your destination. A being who has direct knowledge of Paradise, who represents the Trinity itself, is telling you what to expect. The story of your far-flung career unfolds before you in unprecedented detail.

And it is at these gatherings that you become more fully acquainted with personalities of origin in the central universe—beings who have never known evolutionary struggle, who were created in perfection, who nonetheless find you fascinating precisely because you have climbed from below rather than being created above.

As the Angels

During your time on Edentia and its associated spheres, you occupy a unique position in your long ascent.

> *Throughout your sojourn on the system worlds you were evolving from a near-animal to a morontia creature; you were more material than spiritual. On the Salvington spheres you will be evolving from a morontia being to the status of a true spirit; you will be more spiritual than material. But on Edentia, ascenders are midway between their former and their future estates, midway in their passage from evolutionary animal to ascending spirit. During your whole stay on Edentia and its worlds you are "as the angels"; you are constantly progressing but all the while maintaining a general and a typical morontia status.*[10]

"As the angels." You are no longer struggling upward from animality. You are not yet transformed into pure spirit. You exist in the middle space—stable, typical, progressively refined but fundamentally consistent. This is why the constellation sojourn is the most uniform and stabilized epoch of your morontia career. You have found your footing. You know who you are. You can learn and grow without the constant shock of transformation.

The Legislative Assembly

Edentia is also where you first participate in universe legislation. The constellation functions as the lawmaking unit of the local universe—the level at which the rules governing systems and planets are actually created.

The legislative body is divided into three houses. The lower house consists of one thousand representative mortals—ascenders like yourself, nominated by their home systems. The mid-chamber is composed of seraphim and their associates, children of the local universe Mother Spirit. The upper house, the advisory body, consists of ten divine Sons of special experience.

Three members from each house form the combined council, presided over by the junior Most High. When this supreme commission approves legislation, it becomes the law of the realm.

You may sit in this lower house. You may participate in the creation of laws that govern hundreds of systems and thousands of worlds. Your mortal origin qualifies you to represent the perspective of evolutionary creatures in deliberations that shape the conditions under which other mortals will live and grow.

GRADUATION

After your sojourn on all seventy major worlds, after your experiences on their satellites, after your participation in the legislative assemblies and your attendance at the gatherings on Mount Assembly —after all of this, you graduate to Edentia itself. You take up residence on the constellation capital as a citizen.

The story of your far-flung career stretches out before you—the universe capital sojourn, the superuniverse realms, the billion worlds of Havona, Paradise itself. You have come so far, and yet so much more lies ahead.

> *And on that day when you are prepared to leave Edentia for the Salvington career, you will pause and look back on one of the most beautiful and most refreshing of all your epochs of training this side of Paradise. But the glory of it all augments as you ascend inward and achieve increased capacity for enlarged appreciation of divine meanings and spiritual values.* [11]

You will look back on this period with genuine nostalgia. You arrived capable of tolerating others. You leave capable of delighting in them. The distance between those two states—tolerance and delight—is the measure of what Edentia gave you.

You carry that capability forward now. It will serve you on Salvington and beyond. It will serve you in Havona, where the diversity only increases. It will serve you for eternity, as you work alongside creatures of every origin and type in the service of the expanding universe.

The gardens of God recede behind you, but you carry their beauty within you. You have become someone who can live joyfully with others. You have learned the secret of pleasant and profitable interrelationship.

And that secret, once learned, can never be unlearned.

6

THE LOCAL UNIVERSE

THE CREATOR'S DOMAIN

You were born into a universe, but you understood almost nothing about it. You saw stars in the night sky—distant points of light, beautiful and mysterious, scattered randomly across the darkness like seeds spilled from a careless hand.

But those stars are not random. They belong to systems, and those systems belong to constellations, and those constellations belong to universes—each level coordinating the one below, all of it designed to bring creatures like you from the darkness of space into the light of endless life.

You live—you have always lived—in a *local universe*. Not the entire cosmos, but a defined region of it, a distinct realm with its own government, its own Creator, its own destiny. And this local universe is not just your home. It is your training ground, your school, your partner in the grand experiment of becoming.

THE ARCHITECTURE OF CREATION

A local universe contains around ten million inhabited worlds upon completion. Let that number sit with you for a moment. Ten million planets where beings like you—though different in biology, in culture, in history—are living, working, growing, making the same essential journey from mortality to life everlasting.

> *The organization of planetary abodes is still progressing, for this universe is, indeed, a young cluster in the starry and planetary realms. At the last registry there were 3,840,101 inhabited planets.*[1]

Earth is one world among millions here. Not the first, not the most advanced, not the center. Just one note in an endless symphony.

These worlds are organized into systems of roughly one thousand worlds each. The local system to which Earth belongs is young, still forming—about half of its one thousand worlds have yet to develop intelligent life. But it is your neighborhood, the immediate cosmic community you belong to.

> *Your world is is number 606 in the planetary group, or system. This system has at present 619 inhabited worlds, and more than two hundred additional planets are evolving favorably toward becoming inhabited worlds at some future time.*[2]

One hundred of these systems form a constellation, approximately one hundred thousand inhabited worlds when fully settled. It has headquarters worlds, administrative sectors, training spheres—an entire government devoted to coordinating the growth of millions of beings across thousands of planets.

And one hundred constellations form our local universe. Ten thousand systems. Ten million worlds when complete. A large region of space containing everything necessary for billions of ascending mortals to climb from death to glory.

This is your cosmic locale. This is home for a while.

THE CREATOR SON

The Creator Sons are the makers and rulers of the local universes of time and space. They are of dual origin, embodying the characteristics of God the Father and God the Son. But each Creator Son is different from every other; each is unique in nature as well as in personality; each is the "only-begotten Son" of the perfect deity ideal of his origin.[3]

Our universe is not an accident. It was not generated by random cosmic processes, not assembled by committee, not the unintended byproduct of some larger system.

It was *created*, deliberately, by a Creator Son—a being of divine magnificence, unending compassion, and boundless love.

The Paradise Sons of the primary order are the designers, creators, builders, and administrators of their respective domains, the local universes of time and space, the basic creative units of the seven evolutionary superuniverses.[4]

He is not the Universal Father—not the infinite God beyond all time and space. He is a *Son* of that Father, sent forth to create and administer a local universe, to bring order to space and time, to provide the framework within which beings like you can grow from mortality to divinity.

He is neither absent nor an impersonal force. He knows every world in his universe. He cares about every ascending mortal, whether still on the world on their nativity or scaling the worlds on high. He is present on the headquarters world of this universe, accessible to those who reach that height.

To the children of a local universe a Paradise Son is, to all practical intents and purposes, God. He is the local universe personification of the Universal Father and the Eternal Son.[5]

And this divine Creator has been to your world. Not as a god remaining safely in the heavenly dimensions, but as a mortal, living an actual human life under the same conditions you faced. He has known hunger, fatigue, pain, and death. He has experienced what you experienced—not from the outside looking in, but from the inside, as one of you.

> *It is of record that the divine Son of last appearance on your planet was a Paradise Creator Son who had completed six phases of his bestowal career; consequently, when he gave up the conscious grasp of the incarnated life on Earth, he could, and did, truly say, "It is finished." His death completed his bestowal career; it was the last step in fulfilling the sacred oath of a Paradise Creator Son. And when this experience has been acquired, such Sons are supreme universe sovereigns; no longer do they rule as vicegerents of the Father but in their own right and name as "King of Kings and Lord of Lords."[6]*

This is almost incomprehensible. The Creator of a universe chose to be born on your world, to live as you lived, because he *wanted* to understand you from the inside, to know what his creatures experience, to bridge the infinite distance between Creator and created through actual shared experience.

You were not abandoned. You were *joined*.

THE CREATIVE SPIRIT

The Creator Son does not work alone. He works in partnership with the Creative Spirit—the Divine Minister, the Mother Spirit, the feminine deity that breathes life, nurtures growth, ministers to and maintains the countless systems that allow a universe to function.

> *In physical creation the Universe Son provides the pattern while the Universe Spirit initiates the materialization of physical realities. The Son operates in the power designs, but the Spirit transforms these energy creations into physical substances.[7]*

She bestows mind on creatures, giving them the capacity for consciousness, for choice, for growth. She creates and coordinates all orders of angels throughout the universe. She provides the spiritual circuits that connect worlds, beings, and souls into a functioning whole.

> *From and through this new personal segregation of the Conjoint Creator there proceed the established currents and the ordained circuits of spirit power and spiritual influence destined to pervade all the worlds and beings of that local universe.*[8]

Together—Son and Spirit, masculine and feminine, word and breath —they form the functional deity of our universe. Not the infinite God of all creation, but the accessible God of your local region, the divine Parents who know you, care about you, and work tirelessly for you.

When you pray, when you reach upward toward divinity, these are the beings most immediately responsive to you (aside from the indwelling spirit). The Universal Father is not aloof or uncaring, but the Son and the Spirit are *here*, intimately involved with every world and every soul.

The Purpose of a Local Universe

Why does the cosmos organize itself this way? Why local universes at all? Why not one unified creation administered directly by infinite deity? Because the infinite cannot directly relate to the finite. The eternal cannot directly guide the temporal.

So the local universes exist—bounded regions where a Creator Son and Creative Spirit, beings who are divine yet finite, can serve as bridges between the absolute perfection of Paradise and the limited imperfection of evolving worlds.

Also, God loves to share. It's part of the divine nature.

Our universe is a laboratory. A place where beings who start as barely-conscious animals can become perfected spirits capable of standing in the very presence of God.

Every local universe is an original creation, a unique expression of divine creativity. This one has never been done before. Not in quite this way. And what happens here—what you and billions like you achieve through your ascension—this adds to the cosmos what has never existed before.

You are not just passing through on your way to somewhere else. You are *being formed* by it, shaped by its particular character, influenced by the unique creative prerogatives of its Son and Spirit.

When you finally reach Paradise—if you persist in the ascent—you will carry this universe with you. Its stamp will be on you forever. You will be recognizable as one who came from *this* universe, who was shaped by *these* particular divine Parents, who emerged from *this* unique creative expression.

The Diversity of Worlds

Ten million inhabited worlds. Ten million different species, different histories, different civilizations. Some younger than yours, just beginning the long road toward light and life. Some much older, already perfected, serving as cosmic models of what is possible when a world fully embraces divine purposes.

Some are ocean worlds where intelligent life never left the sea. Some are worlds of enormous gravity where creatures are built dense and strong. Some developed civilization through cooperation, others through competition. Some are peaceful, others still scarred by ancient conflicts.

And yet for all this diversity, there are patterns. Universal principles that hold regardless of biology or history. Truth remains truth whether discovered by humans or by winged creatures on a low-gravity world five hundred light-years away. Beauty is recognizable across all species. Goodness, service, love—these values transcend every particular expression of intelligent life.

On the mansion worlds and beyond, you meet these beings from other worlds. At first, their differences startle you. But gradually, you realize what unites you: you are all ascending. All indwelt by the divine. All part of the same universal family.

The differences become fascinating rather than threatening. You learn from their perspectives, their unique insights, their particular genius. They learn from yours. Together, you enrich each other, each bringing something irreplaceable to the whole.

This is what citizenship in a local universe means: belonging to a fascinating community that transcends origin, that values diversity while pursuing unity, that celebrates uniqueness while recognizing fundamental commonality.

The Work of Administration

A local universe does not run itself. Ten million worlds require coordination, guidance, and support. Problems arise—worlds fall into darkness, celestial beings fall into error, individuals need intervention, systems require adjustment.

This is where the great hierarchy of beings who serve our universe comes in. Angels, administrators, teachers, even non-personal orders of beings created specifically to keep the machinery of a universe functioning smoothly.

And as you ascend through the mansion worlds and beyond, you begin to participate in this work. Service is not external to your growth. It's part of your growth. You develop capacities through using them, wisdom through applying it, and character through expressing it in action.

And you *want* to serve. Not because duty demands it, not because reward incentivizes it, but because you have become one who finds deep satisfaction in contributing to this grand cosmic enterprise.

The work of our universe becomes your work. Its purposes become your purposes. Its success becomes your joy.

Arriving at Salvington

Eventually—after the mansion worlds, after the constellation spheres, after all the preliminary training—you reach the capital of your local universe. The headquarters world where the Creator Son and Creative Spirit who made and maintain this entire realm actually dwell.

You cannot fully comprehend what this means until you experience it. To stand on a world where divinity is present. Where you can actually encounter beings whose nature is so far beyond yours that they once seemed almost incomprehensible—and yet who know you, care about you, and have been watching your progress.

Here, the local universe is fully realized. You understand it now not as a concept but as a living reality—an organism of worlds and beings all coordinated toward common purpose, all participating in an experiment of cosmic significance.

You meet beings from thousands of worlds, each with their own story. And you fill with wonder as you find that for all the diversity, there is unity. Different paths, different beginnings, different experiences—but all progressing toward the same heights, all worshiping the same Creator, all understanding that truth is truth wherever it is found.

The parochialism of your mortal existence—the assumption that your world, your species, your experience was somehow central or unique—this dissolves. You are one note in a symphony of billions. Not diminished by this realization, but elevated. Because the symphony is so beautiful, and your note, however small, contributes to its beauty.

The Light and Life Goal

Every local universe has a destiny: to achieve light and life—a state where all worlds have been settled, all systems function in harmony, and all beings cooperate in service of shared purposes.

Progress happens, but slowly—world by world, soul by soul, choice by choice. But progress is happening. And you are part of it. Every time you choose growth, you advance the whole one small increment toward its destiny. Every soul that survives, every world that moves forward, every being that achieves perfection—all of this contributes.

The universe is not static—it is evolving, growing, moving toward a definite goal. And when every world has been perfected and every soul brought to its highest potential, then novel and different wonders will commence. New purposes will emerge, new challenges will present themselves, new adventures will unfold.

You spent your mortal life feeling small. Insignificant. One person among billions, on one world among countless worlds, living a brief flash of existence in a cosmos that seemed not to notice. Now you know better. You belong.

You are not random, not accidental, not unnoticed. You are a valued member of a cosmic community, a citizen of a universe, a participant in a grand experiment whose success matters.

You are small, yes. But you are not insignificant. You are part of something of tremendous proportions, and that scale does not diminish you—it *elevates* you, gives context and meaning to your existence, provides purpose that transcends your individual life.

This is what it means to belong to a local universe. Not to be lost in it, but to be known by it. Not to be diminished by its magnitude, but to find your place within it. This is home—magnificent, meaningful home. You belong here. You are wanted here.

7

THE SUPERUNIVERSE

THE EDGE OF PERFECTION

STAND ON ONE OF THE HIGHER CONSTELLATION SPHERES, WHERE VISION has been perfected beyond anything your mortal eyes could achieve, and look outward. Not at the stars of your local system, not at the neighboring systems of your constellation, but *out*—beyond your local universe entirely. What you see will stop your breath.

Your universe is not the only one. It is one of one hundred thousand destined to form in this region of space. This is your superuniverse —the grand division of organized space and time to which you belong.

You thought your local universe was big. It is a *village* in a territory that spans distances light itself cannot cross in mortal timescales. This is the seventh superuniverse. And you are only beginning to comprehend what this means.

THE GRAND DIVISIONS

Around the central universe the superuniverses revolve. Seven massive regions of evolutionary space and time, each destined to contain one hundred thousand local universes, each organized and administered as a distinct realm.

Yours is the seventh. The others orbit alongside it, each one a cosmic territory just as immense, each containing billions of worlds, each conducting the same grand experiment of taking mortal creatures and transforming them into perfected spirits.

Your local universe belongs to the seventh superuniverse, which swings on between superuniverses one and six, having not long since turned the southeastern bend of the superuniverse space level. Today, the solar system to which Earth belongs is a few billion years past the swing around the southern curvature so that you are just now advancing beyond the southeastern bend and are moving swiftly through the long and comparatively straightaway northern path. For untold ages it will pursue this almost direct northerly course.[1]

The seven are not identical. Each has its own character, its own administrative style, its own reflection of deity. And beings who ascend through one superuniverse carry its stamp forever—recognizable, distinct, contributing unique perspectives shaped by their native cosmic region.

Earth belongs to a system which is well out towards the borderland of your local universe; and your local universe is at present traversing the periphery of the superuniverse. Beyond you there are still others, but you are far removed in space from those physical systems which swing around the great circle in comparative proximity to the Great Source and Center.[2]

You are of the seventh superuniverse. This will be true forever. The character it shapes in you, the wisdom it imparts, the perspective it develops—these will forever mark you as one who climbed through this realm, who was formed by its curriculum.

THE SUPERUNIVERSE STRUCTURE

If your local universe seemed complex with its systems and constellations, the superuniverse multiplies that complexity a hundredfold.

One hundred thousand local universes, each like your own. Organized into ten major sectors, each containing ten thousand local universes. These major sectors subdivided into one hundred minor sectors, each containing one hundred local universes. And the headquarters of the superuniverse itself—the capital world where this entire realm is governed—exists at the center of it all. A place so awe-inspiring, so charged with authority and wisdom, that its very existence can feel mythical from your current position.

> *Uversa, the headquarters of Orvonton, your superuniverse, is immediately surrounded by the seven higher universities of advanced spiritual training for ascending will creatures. Each of these seven clusters of wonder spheres consists of seventy specialized worlds containing thousands upon thousands of replete institutions and organizations devoted to universe training and spirit culture.*

> *The glory, grandeur, and perfection of the Orvonton capital surpass any of the wonders of the time-space creations.[3]*

From this capital, the machinery of the superuniverse is coordinated. Hundreds of billions of evolutionary worlds. Millions of architectural worlds. Ascending mortals beyond number at various stages of the ascent. Countless orders of celestial beings serving, teaching, administering. All of this requires tremendous administration with wisdom, justice and mercy operating at scales that beggar imagination.

And it works. Somehow, it works. Not through force, not through fear, but through service—beings at every level committed to the success of those below them, to the purposes of those above them, to the ultimate goal of bringing every soul to endless life on high.

After you complete your training in your local universe—after the mansion worlds, after the constellation spheres, after your time at the universe capital—you do not immediately leap to the superuniverse headquarters. The distance is too great, the transformation required too complete.

Instead, you progress through the minor and major sectors, stopping at hundreds of training worlds designed to expand your consciousness, deepen your understanding, and prepare you for what awaits.

On these sector worlds, you learn administration at scales that dwarf that of your local universe. You study the coordination of entire galaxies, the movement of energy across unfathomable distances, the patterns that organize chaos into purposeful systems.

You realize that truth is universal, but its expressions are endlessly varied. The path you walked through your local universe was real, valid, effective. But it was not the only path. Beings from other universes walked different paths and arrived at the same essential truths. Same destination, different routes. Same reality, different perspectives.

This expands you in ways that cannot be taught, only experienced. Your mind—already expanded far beyond its mortal capacity—expands further. Your capacity for understanding, for holding multiple perspectives simultaneously, this grows until you can think in ways that would have been impossible in prior realms.

Uversa

Eventually, you reach your destination—the seat of superuniverse government. The place where powers of such wisdom and authority dwell that their very presence transforms those who approach them. A gigantic cosmic meeting place where beings whose characters radiate truth and beauty so powerfully that being near them inspires you to greatness.

You cannot comprehend this world from where you are now. But know this: it is *glorious*.

Here, you encounter the rulers of the superuniverse—beings so exalted, so divinely perfect, that even the most experienced and advanced approach them with reverence. They are not infinite, but they are so far beyond mortals that the difference might as well be infinite. They have existed since the beginning of eternity.

> *The Ancients of Days were all trinitized at the same time. They represent the beginning of the personality records of the universe of universes, hence their name—Ancients of Days. When you reach Paradise and search the written records of the beginning of things, you will find that the first entry appearing in the personality section is the recital of the trinitization of these twenty-one Ancients of Days.*[4]

And they know you. Not just as a category, not just as another ascending mortal among billions, but as *you*—your unique personality, your individual identity. When you finally stand before them, when they acknowledge you, when they grant you access to the central creation—you will know, with absolute certainty, that you were seen, known and loved the whole time.

THE SUPREME'S EMERGENCE

Here, on the superuniverse capital and the sector worlds, you begin to encounter something extraordinary: the Supreme Being—an aspect of deity that is not complete but completing, not static but growing through the experiences of all finite creatures.

The superuniverse is where the Supreme is most immediately accessible, most directly experienced. It is not yet fully emerged—that awaits the perfecting of all evolutionary creation. But emerging, growing, becoming more realized each moment, from eons past to eons hence.

> *If you truly desire to find God, you cannot help having born in your minds the consciousness of the Supreme. As God is your divine Father, so is the Supreme your divine Mother, in whom you are nurtured throughout your lives as universe creatures.*[5]

This is no longer abstract theology. This is lived reality. You are not just learning about the Supreme—you are experiencing your connection to him, feeling how you participate in his becoming, understanding at depth what it means to be a contributing cell in an evolving cosmic organism.

> *The Supreme is your universe home, and when you find him, it will be like returning home. He is your experiential parent, and even as in the experience of human beings, so has he grown in the experience of divine parenthood. He knows you because he is creaturelike as well as creatorlike.*[6]

And this changes how you understand your own life. Every choice you made, every hardship you endured, every small victory you achieved—these were never just about you. They were simultaneously about you *and* about the whole. Personal choice and cosmic repercussion. Individual life with universal implication.

You are important. You are needed.

THE PREPARATION FOR PARADISE

The time space ascent exists for one supreme purpose: to prepare you for the Paradise voyage. Not just intellectually, though you attain much knowledge. Not just spiritually, though your alignment with the divine will be nearly perfect. But *existentially*—you must become the kind of being who can stand in the presence of infinite perfection without being overpowered, who can directly perceive deity without being annihilated by its intensity.

This preparation takes time—ages. You are being refined, polished, perfected—not to erase your uniqueness, but to elevate it to levels where it can exist in the supernal presence of God. And gradually, steadily, you become ready. Not all at once, not in one dramatic moment, but through accumulated growth—you become someone who can function at Paradise levels, who can perceive Paradise realities, who can contribute to Paradise purposes.

The creature who awakened on the first mansion world—confused, still thinking like a mortal, barely capable of grasping the first lessons —that creature could not possibly perceive the Paradise-Havona system.

> *If a mortal could be transported to Havona, he would there be deaf, blind, and utterly lacking in all other sense reactions; he could only function as a limited self-conscious being deprived of all environmental stimuli.*[7]

But you are not that creature anymore. You have climbed through the mansion worlds, through the constellation spheres, through your local universe capital, through the minor and major sectors, through the superuniverse headquarters. You have been transformed repeatedly, profoundly, and completely. You are almost ready.

The Central Shining

From the superuniverse capital, you can sense something: the central universe. Not the details—those await your actual arrival. But the *presence* of it—the gigantic supercreation spinning at the center of all things. The billion worlds where divine perfection is not aspiration but actuality. The goal toward which all your effort has been directed.

> *The perfect and divine universe occupies the center of all creation; it is the eternal core around which the vast creations of time and space revolve. Paradise is the gigantic nuclear Isle of absolute stability which rests motionless at the very heart of the magnificent eternal universe. This central planetary family is called Havona. It is of enormous dimensions and almost unbelievable mass and consists of one billion spheres of unimagined beauty and superb grandeur.*[8]

It is beautiful beyond description. Perfect beyond imagining. Illuminated in a way that outshines all else. And it is waiting for you. Not to test your sincerity—that has been proven. Not to judge you—you have been judged already and found worthy of endless life. But to *receive* you, to welcome you, to show you what perfection looks like when it is not just theoretical but lived.

You have come so far. From mortal death to the heights of evolutionary creation, to the very edge of the central shining. You have become someone capable of functioning at cosmic levels, of serving universal purposes, of perceiving realities once invisible to you.

But you are not done. Beyond the superuniverse lies the central universe of perfection. And beyond that lies Paradise itself—the center of all things, the source and destination of all reality.

The view from here is breathtaking. But the view from ahead—from the worlds of glory and from Paradise—is indescribably transcendent. Keep reaching. The best is still ahead. And you are ready for it.

8

HAVONA

THE DIVINE UNIVERSE

You have run the race of time. You have climbed through darkness to light. Now you stand at the edge of something entirely different. Before you lies the central universe—a billion perfect worlds spinning at the heart of all creation. Not evolving. Simply *perfect* from the beginning.

This is not like anything you have experienced. This is not another training ground for imperfect beings. This is the pattern, the standard, the living demonstration of perfection.

> *This is the one and only settled, perfect, and established aggregation of worlds. This is a wholly created and perfect universe; it is not an evolutionary development. This is the eternal core of perfection, about which swirls that endless procession of universes which constitute the tremendous evolutionary experiment, the audacious adventure of the Creator Sons of God, who aspire to duplicate in time and to reproduce in space the pattern universe, the ideal of divine completeness, supreme finality, ultimate reality, and eternal perfection.[1]*

You are about to enter a realm where everything—every being, every world, every relationship—exists in flawless harmony. Where divine purpose flows unimpeded through perfectly willing channels. Where beauty and truth and goodness are not aspirations but the fundamentals of being.

You have been preparing for this since you first awakened on the mansion worlds. Every lesson learned, every improvement undergone, every capacity developed—all of it was leading here to this moment when you finally step from time to timelessness.

Take a breath. You are about to enter the universe of perfection.

The Billion Worlds

Every world here is unique, original, expressing some particular aspect of divine creativity that no other world quite captures.

There is a refreshing originality about this vast central creation. Aside from the physical organization of matter and the fundamental constitution of the basic orders of intelligent beings and other living things, there is nothing in common between the worlds of Havona.

Every one of these planets is an original, unique, and exclusive creation; each planet is a matchless, superb, and perfect production. And this diversity of individuality extends to all features of the physical, intellectual, and spiritual aspects of planetary existence. Each of these billion perfection spheres has been developed and embellished in accordance with the plans of the resident Eternal of Days. And this is just why no two of them are alike.

Not only will you find undreamed-of changes confronting you as you advance from circuit to circuit in Havona, but your astonishment will be inexpressible as you progress from planet to planet within each circuit. Each of these billion study worlds is a veritable university of surprises. Continuing astonishment, unending wonder, is the experience of those who traverse these circuits and tour these gigantic spheres. Monotony is not a part of the Havona career.[2]

They are arranged in seven concentric circuits, each bringing you closer to the absolute center, the home of the God of all creation. And you will traverse all seven, world by world, circuit by circuit, learning what perfection means in a million different ways.

> *On the seven circuits of Havona your attainment is intellectual, spiritual, and experiential. And there is a definite task to be achieved on each of the worlds of each of these circuits.*[3]

The outer circuit is where you enter—where ascending mortals from all creation arrive. Even here, on the outermost circuit, the beauty is overwhelming. Not ostentatious, but *right*—everything in its proper place, everything serving its purpose flawlessly, everything harmonizing with everything else.

> *Life on the divine worlds of the central universe is so rich and full, so complete and replete, that it wholly transcends the human concept of anything a created being could possibly experience.*

> *The regulations of the central universe are fittingly and inherently natural; the rules of conduct are not arbitrary. In every requirement of Havona there is disclosed the reason of righteousness and the rule of justice. When you arrive in Havona, you will naturally enjoy doing things the way they should be done.*[4]

The native beings you meet here were created perfect. They have never known imperfection, never suffered, never failed. And yet they are not incapable of understanding you. They are amazingly hospitable, incredibly kind, and completely interested in you.

They have what you lack: perfection from the beginning. You have what they lack: the experiential knowledge of becoming perfect. And here you understand why both are valuable. Why the universe needs beings who were created perfect *and* beings who achieved perfection. Why your path was not inferior to theirs but *complementary* to it.

THE NATURE OF PERFECTION

You have spent ages learning about the various aspects of truth, beauty, and goodness. You have studied them as concepts, pursued them as ideals, tried to embody them in your choices and character.

> *Truth, beauty, and goodness are divine realities, and as man ascends the scale of spiritual living, these supreme qualities of the Eternal become increasingly coordinated and unified in God, who is love.*[5]

Here, truth is not strived for—it is naturally expressed, effortlessly, constantly. They cannot lie, cannot deceive, because untruth is foreign to their nature. When they speak, their words align with life. When they think, their thoughts correspond perfectly to what is.

Beauty here is not decoration applied to function. It *is* function. Form and purpose are perfectly unified. A structure serves its purpose with such elegant efficiency that the purpose itself becomes beautiful. A being expresses their character so purely that their very existence is aesthetically divine.

Goodness is not achieved through effort or discipline. It flows naturally from beings whose wills are perfectly aligned with divine purpose. They love and serve because it is their deepest joy.

This is what you've been reaching for—not as an external standard you must strain to meet, but as an expression of what you are becoming. Your true nature, the you beneath all the accumulated imperfection of mortality, the you that the indwelling spirit has been trying to reveal all along. You see it here, in these flawless beings. And you recognize it: *This is what I am meant to be.*

> *To finite man truth, beauty, and goodness embrace the full revelation of divinity reality. As this love-comprehension of Deity finds spiritual expression in the lives of God-knowing mortals, there are yielded the fruits of divinity: intellectual peace, social progress, moral satisfaction, spiritual joy, and cosmic wisdom.*[6]

Where Nothing Is Broken

At first, perfection feels almost alien. You are so accustomed to conflict, so shaped by the friction between what is and what should be, that a realm where no such friction exists seems almost unreal.

Nothing here needs fixing. No one here needs help overcoming their flaws. No problems require solving, no conflicts need mediating, no misunderstandings need clarifying. And yet it is not static. Not frozen. Not boring.

Because flawlessness does not mean changelessness. These beings grow from perfection into *greater* perfection. They discover new dimensions of beauty, new expressions of truth, new depths of goodness. Their growth is not corrective but expansive—not fixing what's broken but exploring what's possible.

Perfection is not an ending. It is a *beginning*—the foundation from which a new level of growth becomes possible, growth that is not hampered by flaws that need correcting, by deficiencies that need addressing, by internal conflicts that need resolving.

You have been growing *toward* perfection. They have been growing *from* perfection. And now, finally achieving what you've been reaching for, you realize that a whole new kind of growth awaits you.

Meeting the Natives

During your long sojourn on the billion worlds of Havona culture you will develop an eternal friendship for these superb beings. And how deep is that friendship which grows up between the lowest personal creature from the worlds of space and these high personal beings native to the perfect spheres of the central universe!

Ascending mortals, in their long and loving association with the Havona natives, do much to compensate for the spiritual impoverishment of the earlier stages of mortal progression. At the same time, through their contacts with ascending pilgrims, the Havoners gain an experience which to no small extent overcomes the experiential hand-icap of having always lived a life of divine perfection. The good to both ascending mortal and Havona native is great and mutual.[7]

The beings who inhabit these perfect worlds were created for specific purposes, designed with particular capacities, shaped for roles in the cosmic order that require impeccability from the outset.

The natives of Havona live on the billion spheres of the central universe in the same sense that other orders of permanent citizenship dwell on their respective spheres of nativity. As the material order of sonship carries on the material, intellectual, and spiritual economy of a billion local systems in a superuniverse, so, in a larger sense, do the Havona natives live and function on the billion worlds of the central universe.

You might possibly regard these Havoners as material creatures in the sense that the word "material" could be expanded to describe the phys-ical realities of the divine universe.

As the worship of the faith sons of the evolutionary worlds ministers to the satisfaction of the Universal Father's love, so the exalted adora-tion of the Havona creatures satiates the perfect ideals of divine beauty and truth.

As mortal man strives to do the will of God, these beings of the central universe live to gratify the ideals of the Paradise Trinity. In their very nature they are the will of God. Man rejoices in the goodness of God, Havoners exult in the divine beauty, while you both enjoy the ministry of the liberty of living truth.[8]

When you meet them, you expect to feel inferior. You are newly perfected. They were perfect from their first moment of existence, long before the evolutionary cosmos came to be. But what you find is a mutual curiosity.

They are fascinated by you. You carry what they can never possess: experiential wisdom earned through applied effort. You are creatures of time who crawled from dust to glory. You know what it costs to choose good. You know what it means to fail and try again. You triumphed over death. You became more than you were.

This is true knowledge to you. You *lived* it. They can only understand it by hearing your testimony, by learning from your experience, by accessing through you what they cannot access directly. And you are equally fascinated by them. They embody what you've been striving for.

> *Ascending mortals, in their long and loving association with the Havona natives, do much to compensate for the spiritual impoverishment of the earlier stages of mortal progression. At the same time, through their contacts with ascending pilgrims, the Havoners gain an experience which to no small extent overcomes the experiential handicap of having always lived a life of divine perfection. The good to both ascending mortal and Havona native is great and mutual.*[9]

There is no envy, no resentment, no sense of competition. Only mutual interest. You complement each other with profound flawlessness.

THE SEVEN CIRCUITS

As you progress through the central creation, you traverse its seven circuits, each one bringing you closer to the center of all things, each one revealing deeper levels of divine creativity.

The outer circuits teach you about perfection in action—how faultless beings relate to each other, how divine societies function, how beauty and truth and goodness operate when nothing impedes them.

The middle circuits reveal perfection of being—not just what perfect beings *do*, but what they *are*, the essential nature that makes their perfect actions possible.

The inner circuits approach perfection of essence—you begin to perceive perfection *itself*, that absolute foundation which makes all particular expressions possible.

With each circuit traversed, your divine consciousness expands. Not just your knowledge—your actual capacity to perceive, to understand, and to hold truth increases. You are being prepared for what lies at the center, for Paradise itself, for the encounter with something so absolute that even your perfected and expanded self will be stretched to its limits.

THE WONDER THAT NEVER FADES

You might think that perfection, once encountered, would become familiar. That after visiting your thousandth ideal planet, the astonishment would fade. You would be wrong. Every world reveals new wonders. Every being you meet expresses perfection in a way you haven't quite seen before. Every experience deepens rather than exhausts your capacity for awe.

This is because perfection is not a single state but an infinite spectrum of possibilities. Just as there are infinite ways to be imperfect, there are infinite ways to be perfect—infinite variations on truth, infinite expressions of beauty, infinite manifestations of goodness.

Every one of these divine worlds will show you things you've never seen, teach you things you've never known, and reveal some facet of divinity you've never perceived. The wonder does not fade. It expands. And you begin to understand: this is what eternity really means. Not endless repetition, not infinite monotony, but inexhaustible adventure—always new lessons to master, always deeper layers to perceive, always more beauty to behold.

THE BEAUTY THAT BECKONS

The central universe exists for many purposes, but one of them— perhaps the most important for you—is final preparation.

Here, you are prepared as a perfected being. You learn what it means to function at heavenly levels, to perceive divine realities, to contribute to incomprehensibly intricate systems. You discover capacities in yourself that could only emerge in the presence of perfection, because they needed a perfect environment to manifest.

And as you near the innermost circuit, as you approach the portal to Paradise itself, you realize that the moment you've spent ages preparing for has come.

To every world in the evolutionary realms, from every sphere where imperfect beings work and live, the central universe calls.

> *The Eternal Son motivates the spirit level of cosmic reality. He exercises perfect control over all actualized spirit reality through his absolute grasp of spirit gravity. All spiritual beings and values are responsive to the infinite drawing power of the primal Son of Paradise.*[10]

Through beauty glimpsed in moments of clarity, through truth perceived in flashes of insight, through goodness sensed in acts of unfeigned love, Paradise beckons. Every time a mortal encounters something truly beautiful, absolutely true, or completely good—they are touching, however briefly, the reality that exists completely in the divine worlds.

They are sensing, without knowing it, what lies ahead. What awaits them if they keep evolving. What will be theirs if they persist in choosing growth over stagnation, being over nothingness, life over death.

The central universe is not just a destination. It is a promise. Living proof that inherent perfection is possible, that natural beauty can be complete, that living truth can be absolute, that goodness can be total. And every being who reaches it, every ascending mortal who finally enters those flawless realms, becomes themselves a living promise to all those still behind them.

You will be that promise. One day you will return to serve those still advancing. And your very existence will testify: The path is real. The destination is real. What lies ahead is worth every step, every effort, every choice that brought you this far.

Continue on. The source of creation beckons. The pattern of perfection awaits. And it is more beautiful, enchanting and soul-satisfying than you can possibly imagine.

9

PARADISE

THE CENTER OF ALL THINGS

THERE IS A PLACE THAT TRANSCENDS SPACE AND EXISTS BEYOND TIME.

Everything you have experienced—from your mortal birth to your resurrection, from the mansion worlds through the superuniverse capitals, through the billion perfect worlds—all of it has been leading here, to this moment, to this threshold.

Paradise.

Not heaven as religion imagined it. But the *actual* center of all reality —the absolute foundation upon which all of creation rests. The Source from which everything flows. The destination toward which everything moves.

You cannot fully comprehend what you are about to encounter. Even with all your preparation, even having traversed celestial worlds and learned to perceive divine realities, Paradise will stretch your consciousness to its absolute limits.

But you are ready. As ready as any finite being can be to stand in the presence of the Infinite.

The Isle of Light

If you had the time and means of passage, were spiritually qualified, and had the necessary guidance, you could be piloted through universe upon universe and from circuit to circuit, ever journeying inward through the starry realms, until at last you would stand before the central shining of the spiritual glory of the Universal Father.[1]

Paradise is not a world like the ones you have known. It does not orbit anything. It does not spin through space. It is space's center—the fixed point around which everything else revolves. It exists in a category beyond the physical, beyond even the spiritual as you have come to understand it. It is absolute—unchanging, everlasting, the one thing in all existence that just is, without qualification, without limitation, without any reference to anything beyond itself.

Paradise is the eternal center of the universe of universes and the abiding place of the Universal Father, the Eternal Son, the Infinite Spirit, and their divine co-ordinates and associates. This central Isle is the most gigantic organized body of cosmic reality in all the master universe.[2]

And yet it is not theoretical. It has geography. It has form. Paradise is not spherical like the worlds you have known—it is ellipsoid, essentially flat, one-sixth longer in its north-south diameter than in its east-west diameter. The distance from its upper surface to its lower surface is one-tenth that of its east-west diameter. These proportions are not arbitrary; they establish absolute direction in the master universe. Paradise is the cosmic reference point by which all other locations are measured.

The Isle is composed of a substance found nowhere else in existence —a single form of materialization that is neither dead nor alive. It is the original nonspiritual expression of the First Source and Center, a homogeneous organization of space potency not to be found elsewhere in all the wide universe of universes.

Paradise is geographically divided into three domains: upper Paradise, peripheral Paradise, and nether Paradise. Each serves a distinct cosmic function.

Nether Paradise is where the energies of creation originate. All the physical universes, all the material realms, all the energy that becomes matter and life and mind—this flows from nether Paradise. Personalities do not sojourn there; it has nothing whatever to do with the affairs of spirit intelligences. It is the impersonal foundation of all physical reality.

> *The inner zone of this force center seems to act as a gigantic heart whose pulsations direct currents to the outermost borders of physical space.*[3]

The mother force of space flows in at the south and out at the north through a circulatory system concerned with the diffusion of cosmic energy. All force-energy originally proceeds from nether Paradise and will eventually return thereto following the completion of its space circuit. The universe breathes—a two-billion-year cycle of expansion and contraction, and nether Paradise is the pump that drives it all.

Peripheral Paradise is where you will arrive. The peripheral surface contains the landing and dispatching fields for spirit personalities— the cosmic ports where travelers from across creation come and go. Here the Seven Supreme Power Directors maintain their force-focal headquarters, marking the locations of seven flash stations that disperse Paradise energies to the seven superuniverses. Here also are the enormous historic and prophetic exhibit areas—records of every local universe in time and space.

Upper Paradise is where deity dwells. Where the Universal Father, the Eternal Son, the Infinite Spirit—the three persons of absolute divinity —actually are. Present. Accessible. There.

> *God dwells, has dwelt, and everlastingly will dwell in this same central and eternal abode. We have always found him there and*

always will. The Universal Father is cosmically focalized, spiritually personalized, and geographically resident at this center of the universe of universes.[4]

On upper Paradise there are three grand spheres of activity: the Deity presence, the Most Holy Sphere, and the Holy Area.

At the very center of the upper surface, the personal presence of the Universal Father is resident. This Paradise presence of the Father is immediately surrounded by the personal presence of the Eternal Son, while they are both invested by the unspeakable glory of the Infinite Spirit.

Immediately surrounding the presence of the Deities is the Most Holy Sphere, reserved for worship, trinitization, and high spiritual attainment. There are no material structures nor purely intellectual creations in this zone—they could not exist there. This realm is wholly spiritual.

The Holy Area is the residential region, divided into seven concentric zones—often designated "the Father's Paradise mansions." The second zone is your zone: the residential area for natives of the seven superuniverses of time and space, subdivided into seven immense divisions, one for each superuniverse. Each division is subdivided into residential units suitable for the lodgment headquarters of one billion glorified individual working groups. And this staggering number of residential designations occupies considerably less than one percent of the assigned area of the Holy Land. There is still plenty of room for those who are on their way inward—even for those who shall not start the Paradise climb until the times of the eternal future.

And you—the former human, the one who once lived and died on a small world in the outer reaches of an evolutionary universe—are about to stand there. In the presence of the Gods of creation. At the center of all things and beings. At the source of it all.

THE WORK ON PARADISE

Paradise is not a retirement home. It is not the end of activity, the beginning of eternal rest. Yes, there is rest—profound, nourishing rest unlike anything you experienced in lower realms. But there is also *work*.

The finaliters (former mortals who have attained the Father) serve on Paradise, in Havona, and in the time space creations in various capacities. Some teach newly arriving ascenders, helping them adjust to Paradise realities. Some work in administration, contributing their hard-won wisdom to the governments of the universes. Some engage in worship so profound, so focused, that it becomes itself a form of cosmic service.

And you learn that work at this level is not draining. It is not obligation grudgingly fulfilled. It is pure joy—the exercise of perfected capacities in perfect environments for perfect purposes.

You create from abundance—beauty flowing naturally from beings who have become beauty's living embodiment. You contemplate. Not striving to understand, but perceiving with clarity you could never achieve in lower realms. You relate. Deep, rich friendships with beings from across the cosmos, connections that will endure forever.

This is what perfected life looks like. Not static existence, not frozen unchanging eternity, but dynamic, creative, joyful participation in purposes you were made for.

THE PERFECTION THAT GROWS

Here is the paradox: even on Paradise, even in perfection, you continue to *grow*. Not from imperfection toward perfection—that journey is complete. But from perfection into *greater depths* of perfection. There are capacities you develop here that were impossible before. Insights that become accessible only when consciousness reaches Paradise levels. Relationships that can only form between completed beings.

Notwithstanding that these ascendant mortals have attained Paradise, have been mustered into the Corps of the Finality, and have been sent back in large numbers to participate in the conduct of local universes and to assist in the administration of superuniverse affairs—in the face of even this apparent destiny, there remains the significant fact that they are of record as only sixth-stage spirits.[5]

You will never stop exploring. Never stop learning. Never reach some final state where nothing new is possible. The depths of the universe of universes are infinite, and you have forever to traverse them.

We do not know the "finality destiny" of the ascendant mortals of time. At present they reside on Paradise and temporarily serve in the Corps of Light and Life, but such a tremendous course of ascendant training and such lengthy universe discipline must be designed to qualify them for even greater tests of trust and more sublime services of responsibility.[6]

The true state of eternity is endless life full of inexhaustible adventure, new wonders to behold, deeper dimensions to explore, with dynamic participation in realities that expand faster than you can fully grasp them.

The mortal finaliters have fully complied with the injunction of the ages, "Be you perfect"; they have ascended the universal path of mortal attainment; they have found God, and they have been duly inducted into the Corps of the Finality. Such beings have attained the present limit of spirit progression but not finality of ultimate spirit status. They have achieved the present limit of creature perfection but not finality of creature service. They have experienced the fullness of Deity worship but not finality of experiential Deity attainment.[7]

THE MYSTERY OF DESTINY

What comes after Paradise? What lies beyond this first great completion? The truth is that no one really knows. Even beings who have existed since creation began cannot say with certainty what comes next.

There are intimations of purposes so expansive that even Paradise seems merely preparatory for them. The uninhabited outer space levels—massive regions beyond the time-space creations, destined for unimaginable glory. The completion of the Supreme Being—the moment when all finite experience achieves its destiny, actualizing former potentials and initiating new ones.

There is a definite and divine purpose in all this morontia and subsequent spirit scheme of mortal progression, this elaborate universe training school for ascending creatures. It is the design of the Creators to afford the creatures of time a graduated opportunity to master the details of the operation and administration of the grand universe, and this long course of training is best carried forward by having the surviving mortal climb up gradually and by actual participation in every step of the ascent.

The mortal-survival plan has a practical and serviceable objective; you are not the recipients of all this divine labor and painstaking training only that you may survive just to enjoy endless bliss and eternal ease. There is a goal of transcendent service concealed beyond the horizon of the present universe age. If the Gods designed merely to take you on one long and eternal joy excursion, they certainly would not so largely turn the whole universe into one vast and intricate practical training school, requisition a substantial part of the celestial creation as teachers and instructors, and then spend ages upon ages piloting you, one by one, through this gigantic universe school of experiential training.

The furtherance of the scheme of mortal progression seems to be one of the chief businesses of the present organized universe, and the majority of innumerable orders of created intelligences are either directly or indirectly engaged in advancing some phase of this progressive perfection plan.

You are being prepared for *something*. The entire journey is training, preparation, qualification for some cosmic purpose not yet fully revealed. And you are content with this mystery. You do not need to know the destination to appreciate the journey. You do not need to understand the final purpose to pour yourself fully into present service.

The universe has proven itself trustworthy. The promises made have been kept. The path followed has led somewhere real, somewhere marvelous. Whatever comes next will be good. Will be right. Will be worth whatever it requires.

THE GRATITUDE

Standing on Paradise, finally arriving triumphant at the center of all things, you feel the rise of victory within you. You made it. Against all odds—mortal fragility, spiritual immaturity, finite limitation—you made it. From the obscurity of mortal death to the wonders of Paradise glory. From nascent animal consciousness to perfected spiritual awareness. From the very bottom to the absolute top.

And you were helped. Every step of the way. Seraphic guardians protecting you. Teachers instructing you. The indwelling spirit guiding you. The Creator Son knowing you. The Father loving you.

You were never alone. Never abandoned. Never truly lost even when you felt most lost. And now, standing here, carrying within yourself the full journey from mortality to divinity, you understand: it was all real. The promises kept, the hopes vindicated, the faith justified.

> *And when such an animal-origin being does stand, as countless numbers now do, before the Gods on Paradise, having ascended from the lowly spheres of space, such an achievement represents the reality of a spiritual transformation bordering on the limits of supremacy.[9]*

Death was not the end. It was the beginning. You made it. You are home. Finally, fully, forever home. And the gratitude you feel—for the journey, for the arrival, for everything that made both possible—this gratitude will fuel you forever.

> *The last rest of time has been enjoyed; the last transition sleep has been experienced; now you awake to life everlasting on the shores of the eternal abode. "And there shall be no more sleep. The presence of God and his Son are before you, and you are eternally his servants; you have seen his face, and his name is your spirit. There shall be no night there; and they need no light of the sun, for the Great Source and Center gives them light; they shall live forever and ever. And God shall wipe away all tears from their eyes; there shall be no more death, neither sorrow nor crying, neither shall there be any more pain, for the former things have passed away."[10]*

This is Paradise. The majestic center of all things. The transcendent goal of your long ascent.

You have seen the destination. From the mansion worlds through every ascending sphere to Paradise itself—you know now where the path leads. But perhaps you are wondering: How? How does a mortal creature actually traverse this impossible distance? How does flesh become spirit? How does the limited become unlimited?

10

THE GODS OF PARADISE

You have arrived. After ages of ascent—from the mansion worlds through the constellation spheres, through the local universe capital and the superuniverse training worlds, through all billion perfect spheres of the central creation—you stand at last on Paradise itself. The center of all things. The source from which everything flows. The destination toward which everything moves.

And now you are about to meet them. The Gods.

Not abstractions. Not principles. Not forces or energies or cosmic laws. Persons. Three infinite persons who together constitute the divine reality from which all creation springs. The Father, the Son, the Spirit—and the Trinity they form when functioning as one.

You cannot fully comprehend what you are about to encounter. Even with all your preparation, even having traversed countless celestial worlds and learned to perceive divine realities, this will stretch your consciousness to its absolute limits. But you are ready to stand in the presence of the Infinite.

The Infinite Spirit

The first of the Paradise Deities you encounter is the Infinite Spirit. This may surprise you—you might have expected to meet the Father first, or perhaps the Son. But there is wisdom in this sequence. The Spirit is the most immediately accessible of the three, the one whose ministry you have experienced most directly throughout your entire ascent.

At the center of all things the Infinite Spirit is the first of the Paradise Deities to be attained by the ascending pilgrims. The Third Person enshrouds the Second and the First Persons and therefore must always be first recognized by all who are candidates for presentation to the Son and his Father.[1]

Think back over your journey. Every angel who guided you. Every celestial teacher who instructed you. Every ministering spirit who helped you adjust to new realms. All of them were children of the Infinite Spirit, expressions of his vast family of divine ministers. The "living ladder" by which you climbed from chaos to glory—this was his creation, his gift, his tireless ministry made manifest.

These spirit beings constitute the living ladder whereby mortal man climbs from chaos to glory.[2]

And now you meet the source of all that ministry. The God of Action. The Conjoint Actor. The one who does, who administers, who actualizes what the Father conceives and the Son expresses.

His origin is the most dramatic story in all existence. In the dawn of eternity, the Father and the Son became infinitely cognizant of their mutual interdependence. They entered into an eternal covenant of divine partnership. And in that moment—

The God of Action functions and the dead vaults of space are astir. One billion perfect spheres flash into existence.[3]

The central universe itself came into being with his appearance. He is the activator, the executor, the one who transforms divine thought into cosmic reality. Paradise is the pattern of infinity; the Infinite Spirit is the one who brings that pattern to life.

> *The Infinite Spirit, as a universe revelation of divinity, is unsearchable and utterly beyond human comprehension. To sense the absoluteness of the Spirit, you need only contemplate the infinity of the Universal Father and stand in awe before the eternity of the Original Son.*[4]

Yet for all his incomprehensibility, he is not unapproachable. He is a true personality, capable of relationship, capable of love.

> *The Infinite Spirit is a universe presence, an eternal action, a cosmic power, a holy influence, and a universal mind; he is all of these and infinitely more, but he is also a true and divine personality.*[5]

> *The love of the Spirit is real, as also are his sorrows.*[6]

He is the source of all mind throughout creation. Every thought you have ever had, every insight, every moment of understanding—all of it flows from circuits that originate in him. He is the intellectual center of the universe of universes.

> *The Third Source and Center is infinite in mind. If the universe should grow to infinity, still his mind potential would be adequate to endow limitless numbers of creatures with suitable minds.*[7]

And he is love applied to creation—the ministry of divine love made practical, made tangible, made available to every creature in existence.

> *God is love, the Son is mercy, the Spirit is ministry—the ministry of divine love and endless mercy to all intelligent creation. The Spirit is the personification of the Father's love and the Son's mercy; in him*

are they eternally united for universal service. The Spirit is love applied to the creature creation, the combined love of the Father and the Son.[8]

Standing before him now, you understand why he was first. He prepared you for this moment. His ministers guided every step. His mind circuits illuminated every insight. His love sustained you through every trial. Meeting him is not encountering a stranger but recognizing the source of a presence you have felt throughout your entire existence.

On Earth the Infinite Spirit is known as an omnipresent influence, a universal presence, but in Havona you shall know him as a personal presence of actual ministry.[9]

Now you know him face to face.

THE ETERNAL SON

From the Infinite Spirit, you are brought into the presence of the Eternal Son—the Second Person of the Trinity, the divine Word, the absolute expression of the Father's infinite thought.

If the Spirit has been your guide throughout the ascent, the Son has been your destination. His spiritual gravity has been pulling you Paradiseward since your first stirring of spiritual aspiration. Every genuine spiritual value you ever experienced, every moment when your soul reached upward—all of this was response to his drawing power.

The pure and universal spirit gravity of all creation, this exclusively spiritual circuit, leads directly back to the person of the Second Source and Center on Paradise. He presides over the control and operation of that ever-present and unerring spiritual grasp of all true spirit values. Thus does the Eternal Son exercise absolute spiritual sovereignty. He literally holds all spirit realities and all spiritualized values, as it were, in the hollow of his hand.[10]

Just as physical gravity holds planets in their orbits, spiritual gravity holds souls in their trajectories toward Paradise. And the Eternal Son is its source.

> *The spiritual-gravity pull of the Eternal Son constitutes the inherent secret of the Paradise ascension of surviving human souls. All genuine spirit values and all bona fide spiritualized individuals are held within the unfailing grasp of the spiritual gravity of the Eternal Son.*[11]

> *The spirit-gravity circuit literally pulls the soul of man Paradiseward.*[12]

You have been held in his grasp your entire existence without knowing it. Now you see the one who has been drawing you home.

The Eternal Son is the perfect expression of the Father—the living Word that makes the infinite knowable, the absolute thought that gives form to formless divinity.

> *The Eternal Son is the perfect and final expression of the "first" personal and absolute concept of the Universal Father. Accordingly, whenever and however the Father personally and absolutely expresses himself, he does so through his Eternal Son, who ever has been, now is, and ever will be, the living and divine Word.*[13]

> *Had the New Testament writer referred to the Eternal Son, he would have uttered the truth when he wrote: "In the beginning was the Word, and the Word was with God, and the Word was God. All things were made by him, and without him was not anything made that was made."*[14]

He is the pattern of all spirit reality. Every spiritual being that exists anywhere in creation is patterned after him. He is the original, the template, the perfect model from which all spirit derives.

And he is mercy—the revelation of divine love to all the universes.

> *The Son shares the justice and righteousness of the Trinity but overshadows these divinity traits by the infinite personalization of the Father's love and mercy; the Son is the revelation of divine love to the universes.*[15]

> *The Eternal Son is the great mercy minister to all creation. Mercy is the essence of the Son's spiritual character.*[16]

> *God is love, the Son is mercy. Mercy is applied love, the Father's love in action in the person of his Eternal Son.*[17]

Standing before him, you feel the paradox of divine proximity. He is the eternal absolute, the infinite Word—yet you are standing in his presence. You reached him. He is here.

> *To you of lowly origin the Son would appear to be more personal since he is one step nearer you in approachability than is the Universal Father.*[18]

You have been climbing toward him your entire ascent. As you progressed through the superuniverse and Havona, your comprehension of him grew while your understanding of the Father remained more elusive. This was by design.

> *In the progress of the pilgrims of time through the circuits of Havona, you will be competent to attain the Son long before you are prepared to discern the Father.*[19]

He who has seen the Son has seen the Father. This is not simply poetry. It is the mechanism by which finite creatures can approach infinite deity. The Son makes the Father knowable.

The Eternal Son is the eternal Word of God. He is wholly like the Father; in fact, the Eternal Son is God the Father personally manifest to the universe of universes. And thus it was and is and forever will be true of the Eternal Son and of all the coordinate Creator Sons: "He who has seen the Son has seen the Father."[20]

The beauty of his presence defies description. Those who have attempted to convey it admit their failure.

It is impossible to convey to the human mind a word picture of the beauty and grandeur of the supernal personality of the Eternal Son.[21]

And yet a Divine Counselor who has stood in his presence countless times testifies:

The Eternal Son is a grand and glorious personality. Although it is beyond the powers of the mortal and material mind to grasp the actuality of the personality of such an infinite being, doubt not, he is a person. I know whereof I speak. Times almost without number I have stood in the divine presence of this Eternal Son and then journeyed forth in the universe to execute his gracious bidding.[22]

And it was this Son who entrusted the ascending mortal plan to his divine coordination. When the Father spoke the universal mandate— "Be you perfect, even as I am perfect"—it was the Son who took responsibility for making that mandate achievable.

The Eternal Son is the personal trustee, the divine custodian, of the Father's universal plan of creature ascension. Having promulgated the universal mandate, "Be you perfect, even as I am perfect," the Father entrusted the execution of this tremendous undertaking to the Eternal Son; and the Eternal Son shares the fostering of this supernal enterprise with his divine coordinate, the Infinite Spirit.[23]

You are here because he made it possible. You stand perfected because he committed himself to your perfection. The one who holds all spirits in the hollow of his hand has been holding you since your soul first stirred toward higher things.

THE UNIVERSAL FATHER

And now—at last—you are brought into the presence of the Universal Father himself. The First Source and Center. The origin of all things and beings. The one toward whom your entire existence has been pointing.

This moment was promised to you long ago. Through all your struggles, all your doubts, all the ages of your ascent, this encounter was guaranteed to every sincere soul who chose survival.

> *Your ascension is a part of the circuit of the seven superuniverses, and though you swing around it countless times, you may expect, in spirit and in status, to be ever swinging inward. You can depend upon being translated from sphere to sphere, from the outer circuits ever nearer the inner center, and some day, doubt not, you shall stand in the divine and central presence and see him, figuratively speaking, face to face.*[24]

That day has come. You are here. You have arrived.

> *The Father desires all his creatures to be in personal communion with him. He has on Paradise a place to receive all those whose survival status and spiritual nature make possible such attainment. Therefore settle in your philosophy now and forever: To each of you and to all of us, God is approachable, the Father is attainable, the way is open.*[25]

Who is this God you finally meet?

He is the Source of all that exists—the First Cause from which everything flows. But he is not merely a cause. He is a person. A Father. One who can know and be known, love and be loved.

Notwithstanding that God is an eternal power, a majestic presence, a transcendent ideal, and a glorious spirit, though he is all these and infinitely more, nonetheless, he is truly and everlastingly a perfect Creator personality, a person who can "know and be known," who can "love and be loved," and one who can befriend us; while you can be known, as other humans have been known, as the friend of God.[26]

Do not permit the magnitude of God, his infinity, either to obscure or eclipse his personality. The Universal Father is the acme of divine personality; he is the origin and destiny of personality throughout all creation. God is both infinite and personal; he is an infinite personality.[27]

You might have expected the infinite to feel abstract, beyond reach, unknowable. You discover the opposite. He is the most personal being in existence—not despite his infinity but through it.

First and last—eternally—the infinite God is a Father. Of all the possible titles by which he might appropriately be known, I have been instructed to portray the God of all creation as the Universal Father.[28]

And now, in this moment of final meeting, you experience the truth that underlies all existence:

God is love; therefore his only personal attitude towards the affairs of the universe is always a reaction of divine affection.[29]

God is inherently kind, naturally compassionate, and everlastingly merciful. And never is it necessary that any influence be brought to bear upon the Father to call forth his loving-kindness. The creature's need is wholly sufficient to insure the full flow of the Father's tender mercies and his saving grace.[30]

This is not sentiment. This is not wishful projection of human need onto cosmic emptiness. This is what those who have been in his presence report.

I naturally love one who is so powerful in creation and yet who is so perfect in goodness and so faithful in the loving-kindness which constantly overshadows us.[31]

After all, I think we all, including the mortals of the realms, love the Universal Father and all other beings, divine or human, because we discern that these personalities truly love us. The experience of loving is very much a direct response to the experience of being loved.[32]

You are known completely—every choice you ever made, every struggle, every small victory, every secret shame. And you are loved completely. Not in spite of what is known but in full knowledge of everything.

There is an infinite grandeur and an inexpressible generosity connected with the majesty of his love which causes him to yearn for the association of every created being who can comprehend, love, or approach him.[33]

He yearns for you. The infinite yearns for the finite. The Source of all things wants your companionship, and every being who has stood where you now stand confirms it.

A Divine Counselor who has repeatedly been in this presence testifies:

I come forth from the Eternal, and I have repeatedly returned to the presence of the Universal Father. I know of the actuality and personality of the First Source and Center, the eternal and universal Father. I know the truth of the great declarations: "God is spirit" and "God is love."[34]

I have served as a Divine Counselor in all seven of the superuniverses and have long resided at the Paradise center of all things. Many times have I enjoyed the supreme pleasure of a sojourn in the immediate personal presence of the Universal Father. I portray the reality and

*truth of the Father's nature and attributes with unchallengeable
authority; I know whereof I speak.*[35]

And now you know too. Not from reading, not from believing, but
from standing where they stand and experiencing what they experience. The Father is real. His love is real. And you are home.

*When all is said and done, I can do nothing more helpful than to reit-
erate that God is your universe Father, and that you are all his planetary children.*[36]

THE PARADISE TRINITY

You have encountered them individually—the Spirit, the Son, the
Father. Three infinite persons, each unique, each complete, each fully
divine. But there is something more. Something that transcends even
their individual magnificence.

When the three function together in certain ways, they are not merely
three cooperating deities. They become something else entirely—a
unified reality that is more than, and different from, the sum of its
parts. This is the Paradise Trinity.

*The Paradise Trinity makes possible the simultaneous expression of
all the diversity of the character traits and infinite powers of the First
Source and Center and his eternal coordinates and of all the divine
unity of the universe functions of undivided Deity.*[37]

*The Trinity is an association of infinite persons functioning in a
nonpersonal capacity but not in contravention of personality.*[38]

This is not easy to grasp. Three persons who are also one. A unity that
does not erase distinction. An association that produces something
beyond association.

*It would be futile to attempt to elucidate the Trinity mystery: three as
one and in one, and one as two and acting for two.*[39]

And yet you must try to understand, because the Trinity is not merely a theological abstraction. It is the one inescapable reality of all existence—the fact from which everything else flows.

> *From the present situation on the circle of eternity, looking backward into the endless past, we can discover only one inescapable inevitability in universe affairs, and that is the Paradise Trinity. I deem the Trinity to have been inevitable. As I view the past, present, and future of time, I consider nothing else in all the universe of universes to have been inevitable.*[40]

Nothing else in all existence was inevitable. Worlds might not have formed. Life might not have evolved. You might never have been born. But the Trinity? That had to exist. That is the foundation upon which everything else—possible but not inevitable—could be built.

The Trinity functions in ways that no individual person of Deity can function. Justice, for instance, belongs to the Trinity alone. Neither the Father nor the Son nor the Spirit administers justice as an individual. Justice emerges only from their collective.

> *All law takes origin in the First Source and Center; he is law. The administration of spiritual law inheres in the Second Source and Center. The revelation of law, the promulgation and interpretation of the divine statutes, is the function of the Third Source and Center. The application of law, justice, falls within the province of the Paradise Trinity.*[41]

> *Justice is inherent in the universal sovereignty of the Paradise Trinity, but goodness, mercy, and truth are the universe ministry of the divine personalities, whose Deity union constitutes the Trinity. Justice is not the attitude of the Father, the Son, or the Spirit. Justice is always a plural function.*[42]

Each person is love and mercy. But justice—the balancing of cosmic scales, the ultimate arbitration of right and wrong—this emerges only when they function as one.

This is the great reconciliation—justice and mercy are not opposed
but coincident. They appear to conflict only from limited perspectives. From the Paradise view, they are the same reality expressed
differently.

And here is a mystery that will continue to elude you throughout all
the ages of your endless existence: you will never fully comprehend
the Trinity. Not because you are failing, but because its depth is truly
infinite.

You might expect that after achieving Paradise, after attaining perfection, understanding would be complete. But the Trinity will continue
to reveal new dimensions of itself forever. Each revelation will
produce fresh astonishment. Each discovery will open vistas you
could not have imagined. You will never exhaust the Trinity's infinity,
which means you will never stop growing, never stop discovering,
never reach a point where nothing new awaits.

The Trinity exists because God's nature is to share. This is perhaps the
most important truth about divine reality.

nite is disclosed as the Universal Father, who shares reality of being and equality of self with two coordinate personalities, the Eternal Son and the Conjoint Actor.[45]

God shares. This is foundational. The Father does not hoard divinity but distributes it—to the Son and Spirit as eternal equals, to the universe as creative expression, to you as the indwelling spirit that has journeyed with you to this very moment.

The Father, Son, and Spirit are unique persons; none is a duplicate; each is original; all are united.[46]

This is what you have encountered on Paradise. Three persons, each infinite, each unique, each fully God—and yet somehow one in ways that your expanded consciousness can begin to perceive even if it cannot fully comprehend.

The First, Second, and Third Persons of Deity are equal to each other, and they are one. "The Lord our God is one God." There is perfection of purpose and oneness of execution in the divine Trinity of eternal Deities. The Father, the Son, and the Conjoint Actor are truly and divinely one. Of a truth it is written: "I am the first, and I am the last, and beside me there is no God."[47]

And you—the former mortal, the one who once lived and died on a small world in the outer reaches of an evolutionary universe—you have stood in their presence. You have encountered the Spirit who ministered to you, the Son who drew you, the Father who indwelt you, the Trinity that holds all things in ultimate sovereignty.

You have met the Gods of Paradise.

And this is only the beginning.

But I do not command language which would enable me to convey to the limited human mind the full truth and the eternal significance of the Paradise Trinity and the nature of the never-ending interassociation of the three beings of infinite perfection.[48]

Only infinity can disclose the Father-Infinite.[49]

11

THE DIVINE GIFT

GOD WITHIN

YOU HAVE SPENT YOUR ENTIRE LIFE LOOKING FOR GOD IN THE WRONG direction.

You looked up—to the heavens, to the boundless cosmic distances, to some throne beyond the stars. You looked out—to churches and temples, to holy books and sacred rituals, to priests and prophets who claimed to mediate between you and the divine.

But God has been closer than all of that. Closer than your breath. Closer than your heartbeat. Closer than your own thoughts.

God has been *inside* you. Not as some vague spiritual presence that believers invoke to feel less alone. But literally inside you—a fragment of the infinite, a spark of divinity, dwelling in your mind, experiencing your life from the inside, patiently waiting for you to turn inward and discover what has been there all along.

You are not separate from God. You are inhabited by God.

The spirit monitors are the actuality of the Father's love incarnate in the souls of men; they are the veritable promise of man's eternal career imprisoned within the mortal mind.[1]

The Indwelling Presence

From the moment you made your first true moral choice—that earliest decision that indicated you could distinguish right from wrong and cared about the difference—something extraordinary happened. A fragment of the Universal Father came to dwell within your mind.

> *God, having commanded man to be perfect, even as he is perfect, has descended to become man's experiential partner in the achievement of the supernal destiny which has been thus ordained.*[2]

This divine fragment—this spark of infinity housed in the finite vessel of your consciousness—has been your constant companion ever since.

Names fail to convey what it is sufficiently: a piece of God, pre-personal but destined for personality, sharing your inner life more intimately than any being in existence.

While you were worrying about whether God heard your prayers, God was experiencing your thoughts from the inside. While you were wondering if you mattered to the divine, the divine was *living your life with you*, feeling what you feel, knowing what you know, hoping that you would turn inward and drink from the divine fountain.

What It Knows

This inner spirit knows you completely. Not your public self, not your carefully curated persona, but your actual self—every thought, every motive, every secret hope and hidden shame.

It knows the good you wanted to do but did not. It knows the evil you wanted to commit but chose to resist. It knows your potential, gleaming like gold buried in rock, waiting to be discovered and refined.

It knows you better than you know yourself, because it perceives you from a vantage point you cannot reach. It sees what you could become, what you are becoming, what you *are* beneath the noise and confusion of mortal existence.

And knowing all this—your flaws, your failures, your thousand small betrayals of your own ideals—it has never abandoned you. It has never given up. It has patiently, persistently, lovingly guided you toward better choices, toward truer understanding, toward the person you are capable of becoming, because this is what love does when it is divine: it persists. It believes. It hopes. It endures.

> *As far as I am conversant with the affairs of a universe, I regard the love and devotion of a divine indweller as the most truly divine affection in all creation. The love of the Sons in their ministry to the races is superb, but the devotion of this indwelling spirit to the individual is touchingly sublime, divinely Fatherlike.*[3]

What It Does

The indwelling spirit does not control you. But it *can* influence you. Gently, subtly, in ways you rarely recognize as anything other than your own thoughts. That sudden insight that arrives unbidden? That might be the spirit monitor, offering perspective you couldn't generate on your own.

That quiet conviction that pulls you toward the good? That might be the spirit, strengthening your resolve at the moment of choice. That sense of peace that descends in moments of worship or contemplation, that feeling of being connected to something boundless and good? That is almost certainly the indwelling spirit, allowing you to briefly touch the divine consciousness that shares your inner space.

You have attributed these moments to intuition, to conscience, to your better self. And you were not wrong, but your assumption was incomplete. Your better self is being shaped, guided, drawn upward by a divine presence that has been working in you since childhood, patiently trying to elevate your thoughts, refine your values, align your will with eternal purposes.

Every time you chose truth over falsehood, kindness over cruelty, beauty over ugliness, goodness over evil—the spirit was there, supporting that choice, reinforcing it, making it slightly easier than it would have been alone, helping you become more than you could have been without it.

The Building of a Soul

You are not your body. You are not even, strictly speaking, your mind. You are a *soul*, being built jointly by you and God, constructed from your choices and the spirit's creative endowment, manufactured from the interaction between human will and divine guidance.

Your body is temporary. Your mortal mind is temporary. But your soul—the phenomenon emerging from the partnership between your choices and the divine indwelling—this is what survives death. This is what awakens on the mansion worlds. This is the eternal *you*.

And the indwelling spirit is building it with you in each moment. Every time you align with divinity, the spirit takes that choice and weaves it into soul-fabric, creating a timeless person from the temporal materials of your daily life.

You thought you were just living, just getting through days, just making small decisions that hardly mattered. You were wrong. You were constructing eternity. You were building the person you will be forever, in partnership with a divine presence that sees your potential and refuses to let it go unrealized.

The Divine Investment

People ask: How could God care about me? I am nothing—one person on one planet in one galaxy among billions. How could my small life possibly matter to infinite divinity?

Here is your answer: God does not merely care about you from a distance. God has invested a portion of the divine person *in* you. He has placed a piece of infinity into your finite mind. This conveys that you are important enough that the boundless creator is willing to personally indwell you, to share your existence, to partner with you in building that which will never perish.

The spirit monitor is not an observer. Not a judge keeping score. Not a policeman monitoring your behavior. It is a *partner*—the most intimate partner you will ever have, closer than any friend, any lover, any family member could ever be. It sees through your eyes. Feels through your emotions. Hurts through your pain. Rejoices in your victories. It is *invested* in you in a way that transcends any human relationship.

When you succeed, God succeeds through you. When you grow, God experiences growth through you. When you choose love over fear, God experiences that choice from the inside—not as an outside observer approving your decision, but as an inner presence *participating* in the choice with you.

You are the unique vessel through which a piece of God experiences finite reality. Your perspective is irreplaceable. Your experience has value beyond calculation.

> *Nothing in the entire universe can substitute for the fact of experience. The infinite God is replete and complete, infinitely inclusive of all things except evil and creature experience. God cannot experientially know what he has never personally experienced. Therefore does the spirit of the Father descend from Paradise to participate with finite mortals in every bona fide experience of the ascending career.*[4]

DEEPER THAN WORDS

The divine spirit speaks, but not in words. Its language is deeper than language, subtler than sound. It speaks in inclinations: gentle pulls toward better choices. In intuitions: sudden knowing that arrives without reasoning. In ideals: visions of what you could become that haunt you until you pursue them. In values: growing appreciation for truth, beauty, and goodness that you cannot quite explain but cannot deny.

Most of the time, you do not recognize this communication as coming from anything other than yourself. And in a sense, you are right—the spirit is so intimately part of your inner life that its voice *is* your voice, its thoughts blend seamlessly with your thoughts, its aspirations become your aspirations.

But there are moments when the veil thins. Moments of sincere worship, of deep contemplation, and of crisis that strip away everything superficial. In these moments, you might sense something—a presence, deep and loving, that has been there all along but is suddenly, briefly, perceptible.

These are holy moments. In them you touch the truth that underlies all moments: you are not alone. You have never been alone. The infinite dwells in you, and is more committed to your growth than you are yourself.

The Destiny of Fusion

The partnership between you and the indwelling spirit is heading toward a moment of profound union. On the mansion worlds, or on spheres beyond them, as you grow and evolve and align your will more perfectly with divine will, the impossible becomes possible: *fusion*.

You and God—two distinct realities, one human and one divine— merge into a single being. Not absorption where you lose yourself, but fusion where you become more yourself than ever. God brings divinity; you bring the experiential wisdom of having been mortal. Together, you become something new: a fused being carrying both human experience and divine nature.

This is your destiny if you choose it. Not imposed, always chosen. But chosen by millions who have gone before you, who have discovered that the ultimate achievement of personhood is not independence from God but union with God—a union that preserves your unique identity while elevating it to divine levels.

When fusion occurs, you will finally know the inner spirit presence as it has always known you—completely, intimately, joyfully. The presence that has been patiently guiding you from within will become consciously, fully, forever *you*. Not erasing who you are, but completing who you were always meant to be.

The Choice That Matters Most

Here is the all-important question: Will you cooperate with the divine presence within you?

You cannot remove it—it dwells in you by mutual consent made at levels deeper than consciousness, and it will remain as long as there is any possibility of your survival. But you can ignore it. You can resist it. You can build your life around pursuits that contradict everything it has been trying to teach you.

Or you can turn inward. You can learn to listen to that still, small voice that speaks in silence. You can align your choices with its guidance. You can consciously partner with it in the building of your soul.

This is not about following rules. This is not about earning divine approval. This is about recognizing that you have been given the most extraordinary gift imaginable—a spark of infinity dwelling in your finite mind—and choosing to honor that gift by becoming the person it sees you could become.

Every time you choose truth, you align with your spirit nucleus. Every time you choose beauty, you cooperate with its work. Every time you choose goodness, you strengthen the partnership. And slowly, gradually, almost imperceptibly, you change. You become more than you were.

And the spirit rejoices. Not because it wants you to be someone else, but because it wants you to be *fully* yourself—the best, truest, most splendid version of yourself possible.

THE DIVINE INVESTMENT

You are not an afterthought. You are not insignificant. You are not in a cold, indifferent universe. A light of divinity has taken up residence in your mind, sharing your life, guiding your growth, patiently building from your temporal choices. This is a *gift*—a pure, unmerited, astonishing gift.

The only question is: What will you do with it? Will you continue looking for God out there, never noticing the divine presence that has been with you all along? Or will you turn inward, discover the spirit that dwells there, and begin the conscious partnership that leads to fusion, to permanent union with the divine, to never-ending adventures in an endless creation?

> *This indwelling spirit is the living presence which actually links the mortal son with his Paradise Father and draws him nearer and nearer to the Father. It is man's infallible cosmic compass, always and unerringly pointing the soul Godward.*[5]

This divine monitor has been waiting for you to notice. Waiting for you to turn inward. Waiting for you to realize that what you sought far away has been near all along. It is waiting still. Patient. Loving. Hopeful. Turn inward. Find the God who has found you.

And begin the partnership that will last forever.

1 2

SURVIVAL

THE SOUL YOU'RE BUILDING

You were not born with a soul. You were born with the potential for one. But it had to be constructed.

Think of it: you are creating, through the decisions of your daily life, the person you will be forever. The soul you are building now is the soul you will carry when you awaken to eternal life, the identity that will carry forward through all the ages of your endless existence.

This should terrify and exhilarate you in equal measure.

Terrify, because it means your choices matter absolutely. You are not a passenger in your own life, waiting to see what happens to you. You are the architect, the builder, the artist—and what you create, you become.

Exhilarate, because it means you are not trapped by your beginnings. The person you were born as—shaped by genetics and circumstance—this is not the person you must remain. You can *build* yourself into that which reflects not your origins but your aspirations.

Material mind is the arena in which human personalities live, are self-conscious, make decisions, choose God or forsake him, eternalize or destroy themselves.

101

It is not so much what mind comprehends as what mind desires to comprehend that insures survival; it is not so much what mind is like as what mind is striving to be like that constitutes spirit identification. It is not so much that man is conscious of God as that man yearns for God that results in universe ascension. What you are today is not so important as what you are becoming day by day and in eternity.[1]

WHAT THE SOUL CONTAINS

When you awaken on the mansion worlds in your morontia form, what will you remember of your mortal life?

Not everything. The process is selective—it preserves meaning more than information. The address of your childhood home? Probably gone. The name of your third-grade teacher? Lost. The thousand trivial details that cluttered your mortal mind? Swept away like debris after a flood.

But the *meaning* of your childhood—the lessons learned, the character forged, the relationships that shaped you? This remains. The essence of your important relationships? Preserved. The values you fought to embody? Still yours. The wisdom extracted from pain? Forever retained.

Your soul is not a storage device for data. It is the distilled essence of your experience—everything that made you *you*, stripped of the ephemeral and preserved in its perpetual significance.

You will remember your mother, because the love between you became part of your soul's structure. You will remember your challenges, not in photographic detail, but as the character they produced in you. You will remember your choices, not as a catalog of events, but as the person those choices made you become.

Everything meaningful survives. Everything else—mercifully— does not.

The Partnership of Construction

You do not build your soul alone. This is crucial to understand.

You provide the *will*—the choices, the decisions, the moral agency that makes you *you*. But the spirit provides the divine perspective, the spiritual insight, the everlasting wisdom that converts your temporal choices into enduring realities.

Think of it as a collaboration between mortal and divine. You choose goodness, and the divine recognizes that choice has value and keeps it. You choose love, and the divine takes that choice and makes it permanent. You reach, and the divine ensures that reach is not wasted—that it becomes part of who you are forever.

Without your choices, the spirit monitor has nothing to work with. Without the spirit, your choices would remain temporal, locked in the dying flesh, unable to transcend mortality. Together, you create something neither could create alone: a soul that is both human and divine, both temporal and eternal, both uniquely yours and universally valuable.

> *There is something real, something of human evolution, something additional to the indwelling spirit, which survives death. This newly appearing entity is the soul, and it survives the death of both your physical body and your material mind. This entity is the conjoint child of the combined life and efforts of the human you in liaison with the divine you. This child of human and divine parentage constitutes the surviving element of terrestrial origin: the immortal soul.*[2]

The Quality of Choices

Not all choices contribute equally to soul-building. Some choices are neutral—preferring coffee to tea, choosing blue over red. These are exercises of will, but they don't add to the soul's substance.

The choices that matter are *moral* choices. These are the moments when you are most authentically yourself, when your character is most clearly revealed, when you are actively constructing your soul.

> *Mind is the cosmic instrument on which the human will can play the discords of destruction, or upon which this same human will can bring forth the exquisite melodies of God identification and consequent eternal survival.*[3]

> *The mistakes of mortal mind and the errors of human conduct may markedly delay the evolution of the soul, although they cannot inhibit such a phenomenon when once it has been initiated by the indwelling spirit with the consent of the creature will.*[4]

Every time you tell a difficult truth instead of a convenient lie, you add integrity to your soul. Every time you show kindness when ambivalence would be simpler, you incorporate compassion into your permanent character. Every time you embrace challenge over ease, you build resilience that will never fade.

But here's what makes this profound: these choices need not be grand. They need not be public. They need not be recognized by anyone.

The small kindness shown when no one is watching? It counts. The truth told at personal cost? It matters. The courage exercised in the privacy of your own mind, when you face a fear and choose to move forward anyway? This builds your soul as surely as any heroic act.

Your soul is constructed from the sum of your moral choices, and most of those choices are made in obscurity, in daily life, in moments so ordinary that you barely notice them as significant.

But God notices and takes these ordinary moments and makes them extraordinary, transforming them into the imperishable substance of what you are becoming.

> *The secret of survival is wrapped up in the supreme human desire to be Godlike and in the associated willingness to do and be any and all*

things which are essential to the final attainment of that overmastering desire.[5]

WHAT FAILS TO SURVIVE

Here is a hard truth: not all choices build soul. Some actively erode it.

Every time you turn away from the higher choice, you fail to add to the soul's structure. Every time you act against what you know to be right, you damage what you've built. Every time you retreat from growth, you weaken the soul's foundation.

These negative choices do not build a negative soul that plunges into some hell. They fail to build anything. They are waste material, refuse left behind when the soul is extracted from mortal life.

Survival requires that at some point—at any point—in your mortal life, you chose something higher than yourself. That you reached, however feebly, toward truth or beauty or goodness. That you made even the smallest decision that indicated you valued the truly valuable.

In so far as man's evolving soul becomes permeated by truth, beauty, and goodness as the value-realization of God-consciousness, such a resultant being becomes indestructible.[6]

This means that someone who consistently, persistently chooses against the divine will may build nothing. They may reach the end of mortal life with insufficient soul-substance to survive. Not because God rejects them, but because they have rejected the only process through which survival is possible.

There are some—rare, but real—who become so consumed with selfishness, so dedicated to their own ego, so resistant to any whisper of conscience, that they effectively choose non-existence. They reject survival, not through a single dramatic act, but through a thousand small refusals to become anything more than an animal.

*Only by selfishness, slothfulness, and sinfulness can the will of man
reject the guidance of such a loving pilot and eventually wreck the
mortal career upon the evil shoals of rejected mercy and upon the
rocks of embraced sin.*[7]

These people do not awaken on the mansion worlds. They simply
cease to exist, as painlessly as falling asleep and not waking. The
universe mourns them, but it respects their choice. Love cannot force
itself on those who refuse it.

This is the true meaning of damnation: not punishment, but non-
existence. Not torture in some afterlife, but simply ending—ceasing to
be because there is no you substantial enough to continue.

*If there is no survival of eternal values in the evolving soul of man,
then mortal existence is without meaning, and life itself is a tragic
illusion. But it is forever true: What you begin in time you will
assuredly finish in eternity—if it is worth finishing.*[8]

But this fate is rare. Because most humans, whatever their flaws, make
enough good choices to construct a soul of survival quality. For the
majority of humans, this gateway is easily passed through. Most
people, whatever their flaws, have moments of deep love, real
courage, and high aspiration. These moments are enough. The
universe is not stingy with salvation. Its lavish bestowal of mercy is
enough to ensure the survival of every soul who really desires divine
citizenship.

*The sovereign Judges of the universes will not deprive any being of
personality status who has not finally and fully made the eternal
choice; the soul of man must and will be given full and ample opportunity to reveal its true intent and real purpose.*[9]

If you are reading this, if you are asking these questions, if you care
enough about the fate of your loved ones to seek answers—you are
not one of these. Neither are those you loved enough to grieve. The

very fact that you loved them, and that they loved you, is evidence that they crossed the threshold.

THE MOMENT OF TRANSITION

Whatever you have built by the moment of your last breath, this is what you are. This is what survives.

The spirit monitor takes this soul-substance and holds it, preserving it through the sleep of death, carrying it forward to the moment of resurrection. With your consent, this faithful pilot will safely carry you across the barriers of time and the handicaps of space to the very source of the divine mind and on beyond.

And when you open your eyes in those resurrection halls, you will be yourself. Changed, yes—freed from flesh, elevated to a new form and a new body, beginning a new stage of existence. But recognizably, unmistakably yourself.

The character you built? Yours. The values you embraced? Still yours. The love you gave and received? Preserved. The wisdom you extracted from experience? Forever retained.

You will not wake as a blank slate. You will wake as the person you built yourself to be.

THE CONTINUING CONSTRUCTION

But here's the beautiful thing: awakening on the mansion worlds is not the end of soul-building. The soul you constructed during mortal life is the foundation, not the finished product. It is the you that was possible within the limitations of flesh—and those limitations were severe.

Now, freed from mortality, you can build further. Higher. Deeper. You can continue constructing yourself into something you could never have been as a mortal—wiser, stronger, more loving, more aligned with divine purposes.

The mansion worlds exist precisely for this continuing construction. They are workshops where souls are refined, expanded, perfected. Where the foundation laid during mortal life is built upon until it rises to new heights.

The Investment of Infinity

The Infinite is invested in your soul-building. A fragment of God dwells in you for one primary purpose: to help you construct a soul worthy of life everlasting. It spends your entire mortal life working with you, guiding your choices, taking the relevant raw material of your experience and transferring it to permanence. It never rests. It never sleeps. It is the purest energy in all existence.

> *Spirit monitors do not require energy intake; they are energy, energy of the highest and most divine order.*[10]

This is not a small investment. This is not God delegating the task to some lesser being. This is God *personally* involved in your construction, intimately engaged with every choice you make, intensely hoping you will build well because your soul has value beyond calculation.

Why would infinity invest so much in you? Because you are not just building yourself. You are becoming what the universe needs—a unique perspective, an irreplaceable contribution, a person who can exist nowhere else and be no one else.

Your soul has cosmic significance because of what you *are*. The universe is incomplete without you, and the indwelling spirit works tirelessly to ensure that you build a soul substantial enough to survive and contribute to the unfolding of eternity.

Forged in Darkness

Some of you reading this live your lives under unusually difficult conditions. Poverty that denied you opportunity. Abuse that twisted your understanding of love. Disease that stole your potential. Circumstances that made simple survival a daily struggle, leaving little energy for soul-construction.

This is not your fault. And it is not forgotten. But do not underestimate what you built even in darkness. The souls constructed under the worst conditions can be the strongest. Difficulty produces character that ease never could. The will to live and remain good in terrible circumstances builds a personality of rare quality.

The good news is that you do not have to be perfect. You only have to be sincere. You only have to truly *want* to become better than you are.

> *The keys of the kingdom of heaven are: sincerity, more sincerity, and more sincerity. All men have these keys. Men use them—advance in spirit status—by decisions, by more decisions, and by more decisions. The highest moral choice is the choice of the highest possible value, and always—in any sphere, in all of them—this is to choose to do the will of God. If man thus chooses, he is great.*[11]

And one day, when you look back from whatever height you've reached, you will understand: those mortal years were not wasted, not meaningless, not insignificant.

You were building yourself. And what you built was beautiful. What you built was you. And it will last forever.

13

THE RELIGION OF EXPERIENCE

You have been taught that religion is something you receive—a set of doctrines to memorize, rituals to perform, authorities to obey. That faith means accepting what you're told, believing what you cannot verify, submitting to traditions handed down from those who came before. This is not true religion. This is its corpse.

True religion—living, breathing, transformative religion—you *discover* from within. Not a system imposed upon you, but an experience that happens *to* you and *through* you.

You do not need someone to tell you what God is like. You have God inside you. You do not need ancient texts to prove spiritual reality. That essence lives within you. You do not need institutional authority to validate your faith. You need only to look inward and recognize what has been true all along.

Religion, when it is alive, is personal. Direct. Immediate. It is your own encounter with the divine, your own metamorphosis through conscious partnership with the spirit that indwells you. Everything else is commentary.

THE DEATH OF SECONDHAND FAITH

You inherited beliefs from your parents, your culture, your childhood training. This is natural. Children must be taught, and what they are taught shapes them profoundly.

But there comes a moment—and you may be living in it now—when inherited faith is no longer enough. When the answers you were given feel hollow. When the rituals feel empty. When the certainties of your tradition crumble under the weight of your own experience and questions. This moment is not apostasy. It is awakening.

You are learning that secondhand faith—faith based on what others tell you, what books claim, what institutions declare—cannot sustain you. It may have worked for a while, may have provided comfort and structure and community. But it cannot survive genuine encounter with life's hardest questions. Why do the innocent suffer? Where was God when you needed divine intervention? How can you believe in cosmic love when the world seems designed for cruelty?

The inherited answers—God works in mysterious ways, it's all part of the plan, you must have faith—these ring hollow because they *are* hollow. They are phrases designed to end questions, not answer them. They are shields against doubt, not engagement with it. And so you stand at a crossroads: abandon faith entirely, or find real faith through experience.

> *When theology masters religion, religion dies; it becomes a doctrine instead of a life. The mission of theology is merely to facilitate the self-consciousness of personal spiritual experience. Theology constitutes the religious effort to define, clarify, expound, and justify the experiential claims of religion, which, in the last analysis, can be validated only by living faith.*[2]

The Religion That Lives

True religion begins with a simple recognition: you are not alone in your own consciousness. There is a divine presence within you, and it is *real*. Not a metaphor, not a psychological projection, not wishful thinking, but an actual divine presence sharing your inner life.

When you turn inward in gentle contemplation, when you quiet the noise and listen, you can sense this presence. Not always clearly, not always obviously, but *sense* it—a companionship, a guidance, a love that emanates from the deepest part of your being. This is where religion becomes real. Not in creeds memorized or rituals performed, but in this direct, personal communion with the divine that lives within you.

You pray, and it is not words spoken into empty air. It is conversation with an intimate companion who knows you completely and loves you unreservedly. You worship, and it is not obligation fulfilled. It is joy expressed, gratitude overflowing, recognition of beauty that transcends all mortal categories.

You seek guidance, and it comes—not in burning bushes or angelic visitations, but in subtle inclinations, in growing clarity, in doors that open and close at exactly the right moments. This is experiential religion. Religion that lives because you are *living* it, not just believing it.

> *Religion cannot be bestowed, received, loaned, learned, or lost. It is a personal experience which grows proportionally to the growing quest for final values.*[3]

The Authority of Experience

No one can tell you what you have experienced.

If you have felt the presence of the spirit in inner communion, if you have sensed that guidance in moments of clarity, if you have *known* this experience—then this is *your truth*. Not provable to others, perhaps, but undeniable to you.

This does not make you infallible. You can misinterpret your experiences, project your wishes onto spiritual reality, mistake psychological states for divine communion. This happens. This is human.

But it also does not make your experience worthless. When you truly encounter the divine presence within you—when you touch it even briefly, even imperfectly—you know what no argument can refute and no authority can deny.

You know that you are not just flesh and brain chemistry. You know that consciousness is more than neurons firing. You know that meaning is intrinsic to living, not just imposed upon it by human minds desperate for answers.

This knowledge, born from experience, is the foundation of real religion.

THE DANGER OF DOGMA

When spiritual experience becomes institutionalized religion, the experience calcifies into doctrine.

Imagine someone has a legitimate encounter with the divine. They try to describe it, to share it, to help others find what they found. This is good. This is generous. This is love seeking to illuminate the path for others.

But then the description becomes more important than the experience. The words become sacred, while the reality they attempted to point toward is forgotten. The map becomes the territory, and people start worshiping the map, fighting over the map, killing over differences in how the map is interpreted.

Meanwhile, the territory—the actual spiritual domain that the map was meant to guide people toward—remains largely unexplored.

This is the tragedy of organized religion: it so often becomes a substitute for spiritual living rather than a pathway toward it. People learn the creeds, perform the rituals, obey the authorities, and mistake these things for actual relationship with the divine.

To be fair, countless sincere souls engaged in traditional religions have rich spiritual lives. It works for them. And praise God for it. But many become religious without becoming spiritual. They believe without experiencing. They conform without changing. And when crisis comes, when life shatters their certainties, their faith collapses. Because it was never their faith. It was borrowed.

Beyond Belief

Faith, in the deepest sense, is not believing what you cannot prove. It is *trust* born from experience. You do not believe that your mother loves you because some book told you so, but because you *experienced* her love, repeatedly, consistently, until it became part of you.

Living spiritual faith works the same way. You develop it by accumulating experiences of divine presence, divine guidance, divine love—until these become as real to you as your mother's love, as undeniable as your own existence. This is the shift from belief to knowing.

You know God is here because you have experienced the divine presence. You know divinity exists because you have touched it. You know the universe is fundamentally benevolent because you have felt that benevolence working in your life.

This knowing cannot be argued away. It is not based on logical proofs that can be dismantled by cleverer logic. It is based on experience—and experience is self-validating. Others may doubt your experience. They may explain it away as psychology, as neurochemistry, as wishful thinking. Let them. You know what you know. And what you know is enough.

THE LABORATORY OF CONSCIOUSNESS

Your mind is a laboratory where spiritual experiments can be conducted.

Try prayer—actual conversation with the divine presence within you. See what happens. Does clarity come? Does peace descend? Do you find yourself strengthened for challenges you face?

Try worship—from joyous recognition, not duty. Do you sense a shift in your consciousness? Do you feel deeply connected? Does gratitude flow naturally?

Try experimentation with virtuous living—choose forgiveness over resentment, choose service over laziness. Do you grow? Does life respond? Does meaning emerge from what seemed random?

This is empirical spirituality. You test the teachings not by whether they match tradition, but by whether they *work*. By whether they produce joy, bring clarity, and generate authentic spiritual experience.

Not all traditions are equal in this regard. Some promote actual contact with the divine. Others substitute ritual and belief for experience. Some illuminate the path toward God consciousness. Others obscure it with irrelevant doctrines and arbitrary restrictions.

How do you tell the difference? By testing. By experimenting. By seeing what produces spiritual fruit in your life and what produces only conformity, guilt, and empty performance. Your consciousness is the laboratory. The results are your guide.

THE PERSONAL NATURE OF TRUTH

Spirituality is radically personal. What works for you may not work for someone else. What you encounter in communion may differ from what another encounters. This does not mean truth is relative, that any belief is as good as any other. Objective spiritual truth exists —God is real, survival is possible, the universe is designed for growth.

But the *path* to that reality, the *experience* of that reality, the *expression* of that reality—these are endlessly varied. Because you are unique, and your relationship with the divine is unique, and the wisdom you extract from spiritual experience is unique.

Spirituality cannot be managed. It breaks out of every box built to contain it. It speaks differently to different people. It calls some to contemplation and others to action. It reveals itself in silence to some and in service to others.

Your path is yours. Not because truth is whatever you want it to be, but because the Infinite can relate to finite creatures in infinite ways— and your way, the way that works for your unique personality and experience, is as valid as anyone else's.

Beyond the Tribe

One of the great tragedies of institutional religion is that it so often becomes tribal. Us versus them. Believers versus unbelievers. Saved versus damned. Our truth versus their error.

When you feel the divine presence within you, when you commune with the living God, you observe the profound fact that this same spirit nucleus is also inside everyone else.

The person you thought was a heretic? They have God in them, too. The follower of a different tradition? Indwelt by the same divinity, just experiencing and expressing it differently. The atheist who claims no belief in God? If they are good, they are partnering with divinity whether they name it or not.

No tradition has a monopoly on spirituality. Sincere seekers in every tradition—and outside all traditions—are connecting with the same ultimate truth, however differently they name it or understand it.

The tribalism falls away when you recognize: we are all indwelt. We are all being guided by divinity. We are all moving toward the same final paragon.

RELIGION THAT TRANSFORMS

Here is the test of genuine religion: Does it change you? Not just your beliefs—those are easy to change, mere intellectual adjustments that may touch nothing deeper than your thoughts. But *you*. Your character. Your responses to life. Your capacity for love, for patience, for generosity.

If your religion leaves you unchanged, if you believe all the correct doctrines but remain as selfish, as fearful, as judgmental as ever, then your religion is dead. It is performance, not transformation. But if your spiritual practice *works*, if communion with the divine makes you kinder, braver, and wiser, then you have found something real.

This is the consequent validation of experiential religion: it produces fruit. Measurable change in character, demonstrable growth in capacity for love, visible motion from what you were toward what you are becoming. You become less reactive, more responsive. Less fearful, more faithful. Less judgmental, more understanding. Less focused on self, more oriented toward others.

True religion is a living love, a life of service. The religionist's detachment from much that is purely temporal and trivial never leads to social isolation, and it should not destroy the sense of humor. Genuine religion takes nothing away from human existence, but it does add new meanings to all of life.[5]

This doesn't happen through willpower alone. It happens through partnership with the divine presence within you—allowing the spark of infinity to shape you, guide you, and remake you from the inside out. This is living religion. And it is available to everyone who turns inward, who seeks deep, soul-satisfying communion, who allows experience to trump inherited belief.

One of the most amazing earmarks of religious living is that dynamic and sublime peace, that peace which passes all understanding, that cosmic poise which betokens the absence of all doubt and turmoil. Such levels of spiritual stability are immune to disappointment.[6]

Genuine faith produces sublime trust in God's goodness even amid crushing defeat. It generates courage in calamity. It maintains poise in suffering. It goes right on worshiping God despite anything and everything.

THE SIMPLICITY BEYOND COMPLEXITY

After all the theologies have been constructed, after all the arguments have been made, after all the traditions have accumulated their layers of interpretation and ritual and dogma, spiritual truth remains beautifully simple:

God dwells within you. Choose to align with that presence. Allow it to guide you. Let it improve you. Invite it to enliven you. That's it. That's the essence. Everything else is not essential.

The doing of the will of God is nothing more or less than an exhibition of creature willingness to share the inner life with God—with the very God who has made such a creature life of inner meaning-value possible. Sharing is Godlike—divine.[7]

What is essential is the direct relationship between you and God who indwells you. This relationship is available always, immediately. You need only to turn inward. To listen. To recognize the presence that has been there all along, patiently waiting for you to notice.

14

THE PURPOSE OF AFFLICTION

Why do we suffer? If there is a God, if there is a benevolent universe, if there is any justice or meaning to existence—then *why*? Why disease? Why violence? Why the death of children, the cruelty of nature, the seemingly random distribution of pain that respects neither virtue nor innocence?

The easy answers—the ones you've been given by well-meaning people throughout your life—fall flat because they answer nothing. "God has a plan." "Everything happens for a reason." "They're in a better place." These phrases, however kindly intended, offer insufficient explanation.

But there is an answer. An answer that, when you finally understand it, converts hardship from a meaningless assault into a fulcrum for growth that you can be grateful for.

The uncertainties of life and the vicissitudes of existence do not in any manner contradict the concept of the universal sovereignty of God. All evolutionary creature life is beset by certain inevitabilities. Consider the following:

Is courage—strength of character—desirable? Then must man be reared in an environment which necessitates grappling with hardships and reacting to disappointments.

Is altruism—service of one's fellows—desirable? Then must life experience provide for encountering situations of social inequality.

Is hope—the grandeur of trust—desirable? Then human existence must constantly be confronted with insecurities and recurrent uncertainties.

Is faith—the supreme assertion of human thought—desirable? Then must the mind of man find itself in that troublesome predicament where it ever knows less than it can believe.

Is the love of truth and the willingness to go wherever it leads, desirable? Then must man grow up in a world where error is present and falsehood always possible.

Is idealism—the approaching concept of the divine—desirable? Then must man struggle in an environment of relative goodness and beauty, surroundings stimulative of the irrepressible reach for better things.

Is loyalty—devotion to highest duty—desirable? Then must man carry on amid the possibilities of betrayal and desertion. The valor of devotion to duty consists in the implied danger of default.

Is unselfishness—the spirit of self-forgetfulness—desirable? Then must mortal man live face to face with the incessant clamoring of an inescapable self for recognition and honor. Man could not dynamically choose the divine life if there were no self-life to forsake. Man could never lay saving hold on righteousness if there were no potential evil to exalt and differentiate the good by contrast.

Is pleasure—the satisfaction of happiness—desirable? Then must man live in a world where the alternative of pain and the likelihood of suffering are ever-present experiential possibilities.[1]

The Necessity of Resistance

A muscle that is never challenged does not strengthen. A mind that is never puzzled does not sharpen. A character that is never tested does not grow. You know this instinctively about physical and mental development, but you resist applying it to spiritual growth. You want a smooth path. It is a natural desire. But it is not what you *need*.

What you need is resistance. Not cruelty. Not arbitrary pain inflicted by a sadistic deity. But legitimate challenge—obstacles that require you to reach deeper than you knew you could reach, problems that force you to develop capacities you didn't know you had, lessons that teach you what truly matters.

This is why the universe is not padded and safe. This is why you are not protected from every consequence of your choices. This is why difficulty exists.

Without resistance, there is no growth. Without growth, there is no becoming. And without becoming, you are forever static—a thing, not a person.

The Varieties of Affliction

Not all affliction serves the same purpose, and it is important to distinguish between them.

Some tribulation is the natural consequence of living in a material universe. Gravity exists, and if you fall, you will be injured. Cells divide and decay. The body is susceptible to illness as a condition of biological life. The planet you were born on is still forming, still evolving, and sometimes its geological processes produce earthquakes and storms. None of this is personal. None of it is punishment. It is part of existing in a universe that operates by consistent, reliable laws.

Some sorrow is the consequence of your own choices. You ate poorly, you ignored warning signs, you took foolish risks, and now you face the results. This is educational. Painful, yes, but useful. It teaches you to make better choices. It builds wisdom through experience.

Some suffering is the consequence of *others'* choices. They were careless, or cruel, or acting out of their own brokenness, and you were hurt by it. This is perhaps the hardest to understand, because it seems so unjust. You did nothing wrong, and yet you paid the price. But even this can have utility, because you can choose what to do with it. You can become bitter, or you can forgive. You can close your heart, or you can open it wider, carrying your wound as a lantern instead of a scar.

And some discomfort is the direct result of the spiritual resistance involved in growth itself. When you try to become better than you are —when you attempt to overcome your your ingrained patterns of thinking and behaving—you encounter internal friction. This is difficult. It is uncomfortable. It can feel like tearing away parts of yourself. But this discomfort is the growing pain of the soul, and it is most valuable.

THE CURRICULUM OF PAIN

Hardship, when engaged with rather than merely endured, becomes a teacher unlike any other. It teaches you empathy. Until you have suffered, you cannot truly understand the suffering of others. You can sympathize intellectually, but you cannot *feel* what they feel. Once you have walked through the valley, you recognize others who are walking there, and you can offer them something more valuable than advice: you can offer them understanding.

It teaches you priorities. When everything is stripped away—when you face loss, or illness, or death—you discover what really matters. The petty concerns that consumed your energy reveal themselves as petty. The relationships you neglected suddenly become precious. The questions you avoided become urgent. Anguish burns away the trivial and reveals the essential.

It teaches you strength. Not the strength that never breaks. But the strength that breaks and heals, stronger in the broken places. You discover that you can endure more than you thought possible. You learn that survival itself is an achievement. You find reservoirs of valor and resilience you didn't know you possessed.

It teaches you humility. When you are brought low, when you are forced to accept help, when you can no longer maintain the illusion of self-sufficiency, you learn your place in the larger web of existence. You are part of something greater than yourself, and this realization (however painful the lesson) is liberating.

It teaches you faith. Not the easy faith of those who have never been tested, but the hard-won faith that persists even when everything visible argues against it. When you choose to trust that life has meaning even when you cannot see it, when you choose to believe in goodness even when you are surrounded by evil, you are exercising a capacity that will serve you throughout all ages.

"Coming up through great tribulation" serves to make glorified mortals very kind and understanding, very sympathetic and tolerant.[2]

A VALIANT PARTNER

The indwelling spirit cannot stop or even materially alter your career struggle of time; it cannot lessen the hardships of life as you journey on through this world of toil. The divine indweller can only patiently forbear while you fight the battle of life as it is lived on your planet; but you could, if you only would—as you work and worry, as you fight and toil—permit the valiant spirit to fight with you and for you.[3]

The divine presence within you cannot remove your hardships. It cannot make the difficult easy or the painful painless. But it can do something perhaps more valuable.

The View from the Mansion Worlds

When you awaken on the mansion worlds and look back at your mortal life, you see it differently. The pain that seemed so overwhelming, so meaningless, so cruel—you begin to understand it in a way that reveals its purpose.

You see how that which broke your heart opened you to compassion you had never felt before. You see how the illness that seemed like pure misfortune forced you to slow down, to reflect, to reorder your priorities in ways that saved you from a worse fate—spiritual stagnation. You see how the betrayal that devastated you taught you about the nature of trust, preparing you for relationships of depth and authenticity.

You see how every difficulty you faced was an opportunity for growth —and in many cases, you took that opportunity. You became more than you would have been without it. The adversity was not meaningless. It was the price of becoming.

And you see that you were never alone in it. That the divine presence within you was *with* you, feeling every moment of your pain, whispering encouragement in the silence.

You weren't being punished. You were being *taught*. And the teacher, rather than standing apart and observing you with detached interest, was struggling alongside you, sharing your burden, hoping that you would learn the lesson and emerge stronger.

The Problem of Innocents

But what about those who seem to suffer without any possibility of growth? What about the child who dies young, who never had the chance to learn from their affliction? What about those born into circumstances so terrible that they had no opportunity to become anything other than broken?

This is where the mansion worlds become not just important, but essential.

The child who died young awakens on the mansion worlds and is given everything that was denied to them on Earth. The opportunity to grow, to learn, to become. Their suffering on Earth was real, but it was not the totality of their existence. It was a brief beginning to a story that continues.

The infant-receiving schools are enterprises devoted to the nurture and training of the children of time, including those who have died on the evolutionary worlds of space before the acquirement of individual status on the universe records. The guardian of destiny deputizes her associated cherubim as the custodian of the child's potential identity, charging the cherubim with the responsibility of delivering this undeveloped soul into the hands of the Mansion World Teachers in the probationary nurseries of the morontia worlds.

It is these same cherubim who, as Mansion World Teachers, maintain such extensive educational facilities for the training of the probationary wards. These infants are always personalized as of their exact physical status at the time of death. This awakening occurs at the exact time of the parental arrival on the first mansion world. And then are these children given every opportunity, as they are, to choose the heavenly way just as they would have made such a choice on the worlds where death so untimely terminated their careers.[5]

Those born into crushing poverty, into abuse, into circumstances that would have destroyed anyone—they awaken freed from all of it. The deficiencies of their mortal existence are remedied. They are given the education, the healing, and the opportunities that should have been theirs from the beginning. Justice, long delayed, is finally served.

Nothing is wasted. Every soul that survives, no matter how brief or difficult their mortal life, is given the chance to flourish. The universe is not cruel. It is patient and merciful. It knows that mortality is only the first page of an infinite book, and it judges no one's potential based on that first page alone.

Choosing What to Do With Pain

You cannot always control what happens to you, but you can always control what you do with it. You can allow it to make you bitter, resentful, closed. You can use your pain as an excuse to stop growing, to stop trying, to stop caring. You can nurse your wounds indefinitely, building your identity around your victimhood.

Or you can allow it to crack you open. You can let it teach you empathy, deepen your compassion, strengthen your resolve. You can take the worst thing that ever happened to you and transmute it into wisdom. You can become, in your brokenness, more beautiful than you ever were in your wholeness.

The Creator does not demand that you suffer. But it knows that in a world where you are free to choose, suffering is inevitable. And so life was designed in such a way that suffering becomes serviceable.

It is not fair. Fairness would mean everyone starts from the same place, faces the same challenges, receives the same opportunities. And by that measure, the universe is profoundly unfair. But it is just. Justice means that everyone, regardless of where they started or what they faced, will be given the opportunity to become all that they can be. And by that measure, the universe is perfectly just.

The View from Forever

From the perspective of eternity, mortal life is brief. A few decades, perhaps a century if you were fortunate. Hardly a moment in cosmic terms. But that moment matters, because it is where you began. It is the foundation upon which everything else will be built.

And if that foundation involved suffering—if your mortal life was harder than you would have liked, if you faced more than your share of pain—then you have something that cannot be taken from you: experiential wisdom.

You know what it means to endure. You know what it means to face darkness and choose light anyway. You know what it means to be broken and to heal. This knowledge is valuable beyond measure, and you will draw on it throughout the ages to come.

Your pain was not meaningless. It was not punishment. It was not evidence of divine cruelty or cosmic indifference. It was the price of admission to a depth of understanding that the universe values.

And when you finally grasp how it has shaped you into someone stronger, deeper, more compassionate, you will be glad that you suffered. You will be grateful for what you have become because of it. And that gratitude is one of the most beautiful things in all of creation.

15

PERFECTION THROUGH IMPERFECTION

THERE IS A SECRET WRITTEN IN THE BOOK OF YOUR EXISTENCE: YOU were made incomplete on purpose.

Not as a punishment. Not as an oversight. But as a gift—the most profound gift the universe could offer. You were given the supreme dignity of becoming rather than being, of choosing rather than defaulting, of *earning* what others were merely given.

This is the paradox: your imperfection is not the obstacle to your glory. It is the pathway.

THE GIFT OF LIMITATION

Imagine possessing every answer before you learned to ask questions. Total knowledge installed like software, complete understanding granted before experience could test it. You might know everything but understand nothing.

Knowledge that costs nothing has less weight. Goodness that requires no choice has less power.

The universe could have made you flawless. What it gave you is infinitely better: the capacity to become flawless through your own effort and choice.

Even those who were created perfect envy what you possess:

> *On the mansion worlds I have often seen dignified officers of the high courts of the superuniverse look so longingly and appealingly at even the recent arrivals from the evolutionary worlds of space that one could not help realizing that these possessors of nonexperiential trinitization really envied their supposedly less fortunate brethren who ascend the universal path by steps of bona fide experience and actual living.*[1]

The Gift of Imperfection

> *The Gods cannot—at least they do not—transform a creature of gross animal nature into a perfected spirit by some mysterious act of creative magic. When the Creators desire to produce perfect beings, they do so by direct and original creation, but they never undertake to convert animal-origin and material creatures into beings of perfection in a single step.*[2]

God could have created you perfect. Omnipotence is, by definition, capable of anything. You could have been brought into existence as a being of pure spirit, instantly wise, inherently good, and incapable of error. But you would not have been you.

Personality growth requires choice. And choice requires alternatives. And alternatives require imperfection. Imperfection is not a flaw in the design. Imperfection *is* the design.

You were made incomplete so that you could have the supreme dignity of completing yourself. You were made ignorant so that you could have the joy of learning. You were made mortal so that you could *choose* immortality—so that survival would be an achievement, not a default state.

Every limitation, every weakness, every way in which you fall short of what you wish you were. They are starting points. They are the raw material from which you will forge your eternal self.

What Cannot Be Given

To mortals on Earth, some things cannot be bestowed, only earned. You cannot be *given* courage; you must face fear and choose to act anyway. You cannot receive patience as a gift; you must learn it through waiting, through frustration upgraded to acceptance. You cannot have wisdom downloaded into your consciousness; you must extract it from experience.

Character is like this. The kind that matters, the kind that lasts—it cannot be created in you. It must be forged *by* you, through the daily choices that seem small but accumulate.

This is happening right now, whether you recognize it or not. In the mundane moments, the difficult conversations, the quiet choices— you are building something everlasting out of temporary materials. Your challenges are not interrupting your growth. They are supplying your growth.

The Spectrum of Reality

You began at the bottom. Animal flesh animated by a spark of consciousness barely distinguishable from your evolutionary cousins. For years you couldn't even control your own limbs. For decades you wrestled with a mind that deceived you and emotions that hijacked your judgment.

And from this unlikely beginning, you are invited to traverse the entire spectrum of existence. To stand eventually where only perfected beings stand, carrying within yourself the experiential knowledge of every stage between.

Those created closer to perfection begin their existence at a higher altitude, yes. They possess advantages you lack, capacities you're still developing. But they will never know what you know. They can descend to study lower levels, to serve, to teach—but they cannot *remember* being there. They observe; you testify.

When you speak of struggle, it carries the weight of conquest. When you offer hope to those in despair, it's not theory—it's the map you yourself followed out. You know the terrain because you crossed it, bleeding and determined and somehow still moving forward.

This experiential authority is something that cannot be manufactured, simulated, or transferred. It can only be lived.

The Unfinished Masterpiece

Every limitation you cursed was an opportunity. Every weakness you hated was potential for growth. Every way you fell short of your ideals was space for becoming more.

One day you will look back at these mortal ordeals from heights you cannot now imagine, and you will understand: this is where you learned to choose. This is where you discovered that you could become more than you were. This is where the eternal you first began to form.

You are not a finished product waiting to be unveiled. You are a living masterpiece in the making, and every brushstroke, even the ones that hurt, adds depth and dimension to what you are becoming.

The canvas is not yet complete. But already, it is beautiful. Already, it is you.

16

THE SUPREME

GOD WHO GROWS WITH US

You have been told that God is perfect, unchanging, eternal—existing in some remote realm, complete and finished, observing creation from outside like a watchmaker examining a completed mechanism. This is only partially true. And the part that is missing is a big part.

There is an aspect of God, a living, evolving deity, that is *incomplete*. That is growing through time and experience. That is becoming more through the lives of every creature in existence. Including you. Your life is not being observed by this deity. It is being *lived* by it. Your trials and triumphs are not merely being watched; they are being experienced.

The Supreme is evolution's goal and evolution's process simultaneously. The universe is evolving toward the Supreme's completion. But the Supreme is also evolving through the universe's progress. The two are inseparable—cosmic evolution and divine evolution, finite growth and infinite becoming, all bound together in a single extraordinary process.

With God the Father, sonship is the great relationship. With God the Supreme, achievement is the prerequisite to status—one must do something as well as be something.[1]

THE GOD WHO BECOMES

At the heart of infinity, beyond time and space, there exists God the Father—perfect, complete, absolute.

But that is not the whole story.

Interlaced into the very structure of the finite universes—the realms of time and space where you live and struggle and grow—there is another aspect of deity. It is an extension of God, an expression, an experience of divinity unfolding within creation itself.

This is called the Supreme Being. God-in-time. God-in-experience. God who is not yet finished because the universe is not yet finished, because *you* are not yet finished.

The Supreme is growing. Evolving. Becoming.

The Supreme is God-in-time; his is the secret of creature growth in time.[2]

And every choice you make, every difficulty you endure, every small victory you achieve—all of it feeds into this sweeping, cosmic process of divine becoming.

When you triumph over difficulty, something happens that transcends your individual existence. Your experience becomes part of God's experience. The Supreme Being *experiences life through you.* Your joy becomes divine joy. Your growth becomes divine growth. Your victory over darkness becomes part of the abiding testimony that light does triumph.

You have never been alone. Every moment of pain, every decision that came with a cost, every effort toward improvement—the Supreme was there, experiencing it *with* you, through you, as you.

This is not observation from a distance. This is intimate participation. God does not merely watch you suffer; God suffers with you. God does not simply approve of your growth; God grows through your growth.

> *As we strive for self-expression, the Supreme is striving in us, and with us, for deity expression. As we find the Father, so has the Supreme again found the Paradise Creator of all things.*[3]

You are not an isolated individual trying to please some imperious monarch. You are a living cell in a cosmic organism that is itself evolving toward completion.

BUILDING GOD

Here is the paradox that should make you tremble with significance: the Infinite needs the finite.

Your life is not trivial. It is not a test you pass or fail while God grades from above. It is the *material*, the actual substance from which an evolving aspect of deity is being constructed.

Every higher choice you make becomes permanently part of the Supreme Being. You are not being judged by God. You are, in a way, building God.

> *When a human being chooses eternal survival, he is cocreating destiny; and in the life of this ascending mortal the finite God finds an increased measure of personality self-realization and an enlargement of experiential sovereignty.*[4]

This is why your life matters. Your experience has *actual cosmic significance.*

God the Supreme will not be complete until the full spectrum of finite reality—from lowest to highest, from darkest loss to brightest victory —has been actualized and absorbed into divine experience.

And you are part of that process. Your unique perspective, your individual choices, your particular experience—these are irreplaceable contributions to the whole.

No one else occupies your exact position. No one else sees existence from precisely your angle. No one else can contribute what you contribute. Your experience is unique, and therefore it is necessary.

The universe is not complete without you.

The Cosmic Current

The final dynamics of the cosmos have to do with the continual transfer of reality from potentiality to actuality. Always will actuals be opening up new avenues of the realization of hitherto impossible potentials—every human decision not only actualizes a new reality in human experience but also opens up a new capacity for human growth.[5]

Nothing in the finite realms is static. Everything grows, changes, evolves—not randomly, but directionally. Toward greater complexity, greater consciousness, greater unity. Everything that exists in time is moving toward the completion of the Supreme Being—the moment when all finite experience has been gathered, all potential actualized, all choices made.

You are part of this enormous evolutionary current. Not swept along helplessly, but participating consciously. Your growth is not separate from cosmic evolution; it *is* cosmic evolution at the level of individual experience. When you become more than you were—more loving, more wise, more thoughtful—you are not just improving yourself. You are advancing the entire universe one increment closer to its destiny.

This is what it means to be a citizen of an evolving cosmos. Your personal development is simultaneously cosmic service. Your individual excellence contributes to universal completion.

The Collaboration

You are not a servant groveling before an untouchable master. You are a *partner* in the grandest enterprise imaginable: the completion of Supreme deity.

> *With man, the eventual fusion and resultant oneness with the indwelling spirit—the personality synthesis of man and the essence of God—constitute him, in potential, a living part of the Supreme.*[6]

God is not commanding you from outside. God is growing *through* you from within. When you align with creation, you are not obeying external rules. You are *participating in divine nature*. You are contributing your unique experiential perspective to the ongoing phenomenon of God-in-time.

Prayer is no longer begging for favors from a distant power. It is communion with a divine presence that is intimately invested in your growth because your growth is part of its own becoming. Worship is no longer prostration before unreachable deity. It is celebration of your partnership with God, gratitude for the privilege of contributing to something infinitely larger than yourself. Morality is no longer arbitrary suffering imposed from above. It is alignment with the fundamental direction of life itself—the great current of evolution carrying all things toward completion.

And the Supreme gives back. As you contribute your experience to the evolving deity, something mysterious happens—you are enhanced, expanded, gifted with capacities you did not earn through effort alone.

> *Each ascending creature seems to undergo a transforming growth, a new integration of consciousness, a new spiritualization of purpose, a new sensitivity for divinity, which can hardly be satisfactorily explained without assuming the unrevealed activity of the Supreme Being. To those of us who have observed these mysterious transactions, it appears as if God the Supreme were affectionately bestowing*

upon his experiential children, up to the very limits of their experien-
tial capacities, those enhancements of intellectual grasp, of spiritual
insight, and of personality outreach which they will so need, in all
their efforts at penetrating the divinity level of the Trinity of
Supremacy, to achieve the eternal and existential Deities of Paradise.[7]

IRREPLACEABLE

In the grand scheme of infinity, you are smaller than an atom in an ocean. Your life spans less than a blink in cosmic time. But you are not being measured against the infinite. You are being measured against your own potential—and your potential is to contribute something absolutely unique.

The personality of the individual mortal is insignificant in the face of
the total of Supremacy, but the personality of each human being
represents an irreplaceable meaning-value in the finite; personality,
having once been expressed, never again finds identical expression
except in the continuing existence of that living personality.[8]

The Supreme Being will contain the experience of *every* finite crea-ture who ever lived. Your exact perspective, your specific story, your particular victories and defeats—forever part of divine consciousness.

You are not replaceable. You are not interchangeable with others. You are uniquely you, and what you experience and choose will be uniquely yours to contribute.

This is why the universe goes to such extraordinary lengths to ensure your survival and growth. Your experience has value that transcends your individual existence.

LIVING WITH THE SUPREME

When you understand the gravity of this, it can change how you conduct your daily affairs. You realize that every significant decision matters because they build an aspect of God. You recognize that you are not facing life alone; you face it as part of a cosmic process, one gigantic team effort.

You have purpose because you are not wandering aimlessly through existence; you are contributing irreplaceable experience to an evolving deity.

There is much to do. The universe is not finished, God is not finished, you are not finished—and all of this unfinished business is heading toward the moment when all finite experience achieves its destiny.

Your effort is sacred. Your growth is cosmic service. And knowing this—truly understanding it—means you are no longer just living your life. You are growing God.

> *No God-knowing mortal can ever be lonely in his journey through the cosmos, for he knows that the Father walks beside him each step of the way, while the very way that he is traversing is the presence of the Supreme.*[9]

17

THE EVOLUTION OF EVERYTHING

ONE DAY YOU WILL REACH PARADISE. YOU WILL ACHIEVE WHAT NOW seems impossible—union with the divine, perfection of character, arrival at the center of everything. But even then, the universe will not be finished. And neither will you.

Imagine standing on Paradise and looking outward, not at what has been accomplished but at what remains incomplete. The superuniverses not yet settled in light and life. Billions of worlds that have not yet evolved intelligent life. Trillions of potential souls not yet born, who have not yet made their choices, not yet begun the ascent you will have completed.

And beyond the known universes, in the vast empty regions of outer space, great things are stirring even now.

We are convinced, from the study of physical law and from the observation of the starry realms, that the infinite Creator is not yet manifest in finality of cosmic expression, that much of the cosmic potential of the Infinite is still self-contained and unrevealed. To created beings the master universe might appear to be almost infinite, but it is far from finished. [1]

Galaxies are forming. Energy is organizing. Space itself is preparing for purposes not yet revealed, for civilizations not yet born, for adventures not yet begun.

Everything evolves with direction and purpose toward greater complexity, greater consciousness, greater unity. You live in an *expanding* cosmos. Not a finished creation, not a completed product, but a masterverse still becoming, still reaching toward its full potential. And you, one day perfected, will be part of that becoming. Forever.

The Universal Principle of Growth

Nothing in the finite realms is static. Everything that exists in time is either growing or dying—and in a universe designed by infinite wisdom, death itself serves growth by clearing space for new life, new experiments, new possibilities.

Worlds evolve from molten chaos to stable platforms for life. Life evolves from simple chemistry to complex organisms capable of consciousness. Consciousness evolves from animal awareness to moral capacity to spiritual insight. Civilizations evolve from barbarism toward enlightenment. And individuals like you evolve from mortality to Paradise and beyond.

This is not accidental, nor does the universe randomly produce progress as a byproduct of blind forces. This is *design*: deliberate, purposeful, aimed at bringing potential into actuality, at transmuting what could be into what is. The universe wants to grow. Is designed to grow. Growth is part of its fundamental nature.

You experienced this personally. You did not remain the confused mortal who died not knowing what came next. You found new life and grew immeasurably greater. Your growth was supported, facilitated, made possible by a universe whose purpose is to promote exactly this.

And what happened to you is happening everywhere, at every level. Atoms organizing into molecules. Molecules into cells. Cells into organisms. Organisms into societies. Societies into civilizations. Civilizations into perfected planetary systems. Everything reaching upward. Everything becoming more orderly, more harmonious, more beautiful. Everything participating in a cosmic current flowing toward completion.

> *There is original endowment of adaptation in living things and beings. In every living plant or animal cell, in every living organism —material or spiritual—there is an insatiable craving for the attainment of ever-increasing perfection of environmental adjustment, organismal adaptation, and augmented life realization. These interminable efforts of all living things evidence the existence within them of an innate striving for perfection.[2]*

THE OUTER SPACE LEVELS

Beyond the superuniverses, in regions so boundless that light from the more distant emerging galaxies has not yet reached organized space, something enormous is taking shape.

Outer space. Four levels of it, each larger than the previous, each destined for purposes not yet revealed. Without life now, but not forever. Organizing now, preparing now, like a womb quickening with life yet unborn.

> *The central universe is the creation of eternity; the seven superuniverses are the creations of time; the four outer space levels are undoubtedly destined to eventuate-evolve the ultimacy of creation.[3]*

What will emerge there? No one knows with certainty. But the possibilities are tantalizing: Perhaps these regions will be settled by beings who never knew mortality, who never climbed from imperfection. Perhaps they will be the native realms of perfected creatures, while the superuniverses remain forever the domain of those who achieved perfection through evolution.

Perhaps they will provide challenges that require finaliters—those who have traversed the full spectrum from lowest to highest, who carry experiential wisdom no created-perfect being can possess. Perhaps this is why you were prepared so thoroughly, why you climbed so far, why you were given capacities that seem excessive for current needs.

> *It is believed that a new type of creation is in process, an order of universes destined to become the scene of the future activities of the assembling Corps of the Finality; and if our conjectures are correct, then the endless future may hold for all of you the same enthralling spectacles that the endless past has held for your seniors and predecessors.[4]*

> *It is believed that a new type of creation is in process, an order of universes destined to become the scene of the future activities of the assembling Corps of the Finality; and if our conjectures are correct, then the endless future may hold for all of you the same enthralling spectacles that the endless past has held for your seniors and predecessors.[5]*

Perhaps they represent evolution's next stage—not just biological or social or even spiritual evolution, but evolution of evolution itself. New modes of growth, new pathways to finality, new experiments in divine creativity.

Whatever they are, they represent an essential fact: the universe is not finished. Creation is not complete. The story is not over. And you, standing prepared on Paradise, are positioned perfectly to participate in whatever comes next.

The Overcontrol of Evolution

Evolution is not purposeless. It is not random mutation plus natural selection producing complexity by accident. It is not blind forces stumbling toward order.

It is *directed* evolution. Not in the sense that every detail is predetermined, but in the sense that the whole system is biased toward growth, designed to promote increasing complexity and consciousness, structured to support the emergence of beings capable of choosing their own destiny.

> *The evolution of life is a technique ever progressive, differential, and variable, but never haphazard, uncontrolled, nor wholly experimental, in the accidental sense.*[6]

Your world evolved because it was *supposed* to evolve. Life emerged because the universe is designed to produce life. Consciousness developed because the cosmos needs conscious beings to experience it, to know it, to participate in its ongoing creation.

> *Many features of human life afford abundant evidence that the phenomenon of mortal existence was intelligently planned, that organic evolution is not a mere cosmic accident.*[7]

And you emerged—a being capable of moral choice, spiritual growth, and eventual fusion with divinity—because this is what evolution was reaching for all along.

> *It is the integrated functioning of the Life Carriers, the physical controllers, and the spirit adjutants that conditions the course of organic evolution on the inhabited worlds. This is why evolution—on Earth or elsewhere—is always purposeful and never accidental.*[8]

Consider the implications. Evolution on your world was not left to chance. Beings called Life Carriers were assigned to your planet. They designed the initial life patterns, implanted them in your ancient seas, and then watched over their development for millions of years. They fostered favorable mutations. They guided the process toward the emergence of will creatures—beings who could know God and choose to seek him.

> *As mind evolution is dependent on, and delayed by, the slow development of physical conditions, so is spiritual progress dependent on mental expansion and unfailingly delayed by intellectual retardation. But this does not mean that spiritual evolution is dependent on education, culture, or wisdom. The soul may evolve regardless of mental culture but not in the absence of mental capacity and desire—the choice of survival and the decision to achieve ever-increasing perfection—to do the will of the Father in heaven.*[9]

You are not an accident. You are the *goal*—or at least one goal among many, one successful expression of what evolution makes possible.

The Eternal Frontier

Here is what excites you now, standing on Paradise with eternity and infinity stretching before you: there is always more. More to explore. More to understand. More to become. More to serve. More to create. More to experience. Perfection is not the end of possibility. It is the *liberation* of possibility.

> *The universe is nonstatic. Stability is not the result of inertia but rather the product of balanced energies, cooperative minds, coordinated morontias, spirit overcontrol, and personality unification. Stability is wholly and always proportional to divinity.*[10]

You will serve in the outer universes. You will contribute to challenges not yet fully defined, participate in purposes not yet fully revealed.

The frontier is eternal because creation is infinite. You can explore forever and never exhaust it. You can grow forever and never reach some final state where nothing new is possible. You can travel forever and never run out of wonders to behold.

THE WISDOM EARNED

You understand now what you could not have understood as a mortal: evolution is the *only way* to produce beings like you—creatures who know what growth costs, but who can testify that the journey is worth it. This wisdom has infinite value. It cannot be created any other way. It can only be earned through the long, difficult ascent.

And the universe will draw on this wisdom forever. When new worlds need guidance, when new beings need encouragement, when challenges arise that require understanding both struggle and triumph —perfected mortals will serve, because no one else carries quite what you carry.

Your suffering was not meaningless, not wasted. Your confusion and fear and pain—all of it contributed to making you someone of infinite value to an evolving cosmos.

The evolution that brought you from animal to angel to Paradise citizen is the same evolution shaping galaxies, organizing energy into matter into life into consciousness into spirit. You are not separate from cosmic evolution. You *are* cosmic evolution, made personal, made conscious, made capable of choosing to participate in its purposes.

THE GREAT BECOMING

How do you live now knowing that you dwell in an evolving universe, that you are part of some great becoming, that your choices contribute to cosmic development?

You live with *purpose*. Nothing you do is trivial when it contributes to universal evolution. No act of service is small when it advances the

Supreme's completion. No moment of growth is wasted when it adds to the sum of finite experience.

You live with *patience*. Evolution works on cosmic timescales. What seems slow from the finite perspective is breathtaking progress when measured against eternity. The universe is not failing because it is not yet perfect—it is succeeding because it is steadily, persistently becoming more than it was.

You live with *hope*. Not blind optimism, not wishful thinking, but grounded confidence based on trajectory observed. The universe is getting better. More conscious, more unified, more aligned with divine purposes.

You live with *participation*. You are not a passenger on evolution's journey but a conscious contributor to its progress. Every choice you make either advances or obstructs the cosmic current. Every action helps or hinders.

And you live with *joy*. Because you know where all this is heading. You have stood on Paradise. You have seen perfection. You know what lies ahead for every world that perseveres, every soul that chooses survival, every civilization that reaches for light.

The journey is long but it leads somewhere real. The ascent is hard but it achieves something eternal. The evolution is slow but it moves toward a completion worth any price.

Everything evolves toward perfection. You are invited to participate in this perfecting. To be part of whatever comes next. To contribute your unique perspective, earned through your unique journey, to purposes that will unfold across ages yet uncounted.

This is the meaning of everlasting life: not endless existence doing nothing, but perpetual participation in cosmic evolution, forever growing, forever serving, forever finding new frontiers.

You are evolution made conscious. Evolution that can choose its own direction, that can knowingly cooperate with cosmic purposes, that can look back at its origins and forward to its destiny and say: "I choose this." And the universe responds: "Yes. This is why you exist. This is what you are for. Welcome to the greatest adventure imaginable—the evolution of everything, including you."

Keep evolving. Keep growing. Keep reaching for what you have not yet become.

> *When spiritual values receive proper recognition, then cosmic meanings become discernible, and increasingly the personality is released from the handicaps of time and delivered from the limitations of space.*[11]

Because the best version of you is not behind you. It is ahead of you. Always ahead, always calling, always possible. Thus is the way of the evolving cosmos. And you are home in it.

1 8

THE CRAFT OF BECOMING

You have seen Paradise. You understand cosmic evolution. You know the ladder with which souls climb from mortality to perfection. But here is the question that brings everything back to earth, back to the daily and immediate, back to the life you are living right now: *What do you do today?*

You are still mortal, still bound in flesh, still facing the thousand mundane decisions that fill ordinary hours. You still wake tired, still have a body to feed, still deal with difficult people. The cosmic perspective you've gained—what does it mean for *this* day, *this* hour, *this* choice in front of you right now?

Here is the answer: your life is art. You are both the artist and the canvas, both the sculptor and the stone. Every choice you make is a brushstroke. Every day lived is a line drawn. Every value embraced is a color added to the palette. And what you are creating, day by day, is *you*. The you that will live forever.

The Artist's Responsibility

Artists do not create carelessly. They do not apply paint randomly and call it finished. They *choose*—color, composition, form, every element deliberately selected to create meaning and beauty.

You have the same responsibility. Not to be perfect—no artist creates a masterpiece on their first attempt. But to be *intentional*. To recognize that your choices matter, that you are a cocreator of your soul, that the person you are becoming is the most important work you will ever create.

You are not a passive victim of circumstance. You are an active agent, a conscious creator, an artist shaping the material of your temporary life into a perpetually enduring child of God.

The medium you work with is your daily life. The tools are your choices. The vision comes from the spirit within you, patiently showing you glimpses of what you could become. Every morning you wake is a blank canvas. What will you create today? What colors will you add to the work in progress? What values will you embody that will become permanent features of your undying character?

The Mundane as Sacred

You might think: "But my life is so ordinary. I wake, I work, I eat, I sleep. Where is the art in that?" Everywhere. In everything.

The way you greet your family in the morning—patience or irritation, kindness or indifference. This is a brushstroke. You are choosing what kind of person you are becoming. The way you do your work—with integrity or with corners cut, with care or with apathy. This is shaping your character, adding to or detracting from the soul you are building. The way you treat the stranger, the clerk, the person who cannot benefit you in any way. This reveals who you are beneath the performance, and who you are is what survives death.

There are no meaningless moments. No insignificant choices. Every interaction, every decision, every thought you dwell on—these are the materials from which your eternal self is being constructed. The mundane *is* sacred when you recognize it for what it is: opportunity.

You do not need dramatic circumstances to create a magnificent life. You need only to treat ordinary circumstances with the attention they deserve, recognizing that the person you are becoming is being shaped right now, in this moment, by how you choose to respond to what is in front of you.

THE PALETTE OF VALUES

An artist selects their palette carefully. Not every color, not random selection, but specific hues chosen to create specific effects. Your palette consists of values. And you choose, moment by moment, which to emphasize, which to neglect, which to make central to your emerging character.

> *These divine qualities are perfectly and absolutely unified in God. And every God-knowing man or angel possesses the potential of unlimited self-expression on ever-progressive levels of unified self-realization by the technique of the never-ending achievement of Godlikeness—the experiential blending in the evolutionary experience of eternal truth, universal beauty, and divine goodness.* [1]

Beauty means appreciating what elevates, what inspires, what touches deeply. It means pausing to notice sunlight through leaves, to hear joyful laughter, to recognize grace in unexpected places. Every moment spent in wholehearted appreciation of beauty trains your soul to perceive it, cultivates your capacity for wonder, and develops your sensitivity to what's important and life giving.

Goodness means choosing what serves others, what contributes beyond yourself, what builds rather than destroys. It means being *positive.*

Goodness is always growing toward new levels of the increasing liberty of moral self-realization and spiritual personality attainment —the discovery of, and identification with, the indwelling spirit. An experience is good when it heightens the appreciation of beauty, augments the moral will, enhances the discernment of truth, enlarges the capacity to love and serve one's fellows, exalts the spiritual ideals, and unifies the supreme human motives of time with the eternal plans of the indwelling spirit, all of which lead directly to an increased desire to do the Father's will, thereby fostering the divine passion to find God and to be more like him.[2]

Truth means aligning with reality, speaking honestly, thinking clearly. It means refusing the lies that soothe, facing facts that disturb, and pursuing understanding even when ignorance feels safer. Every time you choose to see what is actually there—rather than what you wish were there—you strengthen your capacity for truth. Every sincere word spoken, every self-deception resisted, every difficult reality acknowledged builds integrity into your permanent character. Truth is not just about what you say to others. It is about what you admit to yourself. The soul built on truth has a foundation that cannot be shaken.

THE DISCIPLINE OF DAILY PRACTICE

Artists practice. Daily, persistently, even when inspiration is absent, even when the work feels mechanical. Because mastery comes not from occasional brilliance but from consistent engagement with the craft. Your craft is becoming. And it requires the same discipline.

You do not become patient by waiting for the moment you feel like being patient. You become patient by choosing patience repeatedly, especially when you do not feel like it, until patience becomes habitual. You do not become honest by waiting until honesty is easy. You become truthful by speaking truth, over and over, until candor becomes your default response.

You do not become loving by waiting until you feel affection. You become loving by choosing loving actions even when emotions do not cooperate, by treating others well regardless of whether they deserve it, until love is no longer something you do but something you are.

This is why daily life matters so much. Because character is built through repetition, through choosing the same values over and over until they become you. The mansion worlds can teach you cosmic truth, can expand your consciousness, can refine your capacities—but they cannot *give* you character. That you must build yourself, choice by daily choice, in the ordinary moments of existence.

> *The past is unchangeable; only the future can be changed by the ministry of the present creativity of the inner self.*[3]

THE INTEGRATION OF SHADOW

Every artist knows: shadows create depth. Light alone is flat. It is the interplay of light and dark that produces dimension, that makes the two-dimensional suggest three-dimensionality.

Your life has shadows. Failure, affliction, moments you wish had never happened, choices you deeply regret. These are not mistakes in the artistic process. They are essential elements. Do not hide your shadows. Do not pretend they do not exist. *Integrate* them. Learn from them. Let them deepen your appreciation for grace, for forgiveness, for mercy.

A soul built only from easy victories would be shallow. A character formed only in comfort would be soft. The failures and the painful lessons—these add depth and texture to what you are becoming. You are not painting a perfect picture. You are creating an authentic one— a true representation of what it means to be human, to fall and rise and keep reaching.

THE EXHIBITION

One day your mortal life will end. The painting will be complete. The sculpture finished. The artwork that is your life will be...*done*. And then it will be exhibited. Not to judges looking for flaws, not to critics ready to condemn. But on the mansion worlds, where beings who understand the challenges of mortality will see what you built from the materials available to you.

They will not compare your work to some impossible standard. They will assess it based on what you had to work with—your native capacity, your circumstances, the challenges you faced, the resources available to you. Did you use what you had well? Were you diligent, were you genuine, did you exercise sincere effort?

If yes, then the exhibition is a success. Your work is accepted. Your art has value. You have uniquely contributed to the eternal collection of souls that populate the celestial realms.

There can be no handicap of human heredity or deprivation of mortal environment which the morontia career will not fully compensate and wholly remove. At last the aspirations of evolutionary mediocrity may be realized. While the Gods do not arbitrarily bestow talents and ability upon the children of time, they do provide for the attainment of the satisfaction of all their noble longings and for the gratification of all human hunger for supernal self-expression.[4]

19

SEEN FROM ABOVE

You are going to die. Your heart will stop, your brain will cease its electrical dance, and the body you have worn for decades will become an object, a thing, a corpse that others must dispose of.

This is the certainty that haunts you. The shadow that falls across even your brightest moments, whispering: *This will end. Everyone you love will end. Everything you build will crumble. What is the point?*

And if you are honest, there are days when the nihilism feels justified. When suffering seems meaningless, when injustice goes unpunished, when good people die young while the cruel prosper. When the universe appears indifferent rather than benevolent, random rather than designed, going nowhere.

This is the view from the ground. From the limited perspective that knows only what it can perceive. But you know more now. You know what comes after. You know where the path leads. You know that your story does not conclude but continues, that what seems like final defeat is victory's beginning.

This is the long view. And once you truly grasp it, you can never see your life the same way again.

The Illusion of Finality

Death feels final because it is the end of everything you can currently perceive. Your mortal senses stop. Your earthly relationships pause. Your physical existence terminates. But feeling final is not the same as *being* final.

You have been misled by those who could not see beyond death, who assumed that when their perception ended, life ended, and who mistook the limits of their senses for the limits of existence. The truth is staggeringly different: death is a *moment*. A brief transition. A doorway you step through into something larger than what you left behind.

On the other side of that doorway, you wake. You open your eyes. You realize that you are still *you*—not erased, not dissolved into some impersonal ocean, but yourself, recognizable, continuous with who you were. And you see that everyone you loved who died before you is *there*. Not gone. Not lost. Not ceased to exist. But *there*, waiting, welcoming, ready to continue relationships that mortality interrupted but did not end.

And knowing this—understanding it with the certainty that comes from both feeling the reality response of truth observed and more fully understanding the architecture of the cosmos—this changes how you live now.

For Those Who Grieve

You have lost someone. Perhaps recently, perhaps years ago, but the pain still aches. The absence still hurts. The hole they left in your life has not filled, cannot fill, because they were irreplaceable. And you have been told that they're in a better place or everything happens for a reason or time heals all wounds.

They attempt to gloss over existential pain with platitudes that do not address the actual problem: the person you loved is *gone,* and no philosophical perspective makes that absence less real. But here is what you have not been told, what most do not know: They woke up. Welcomed. Embraced. Shown that death was a necessary transfer to a new beginning.

They are learning now. Growing now. Healing from whatever broke them in mortal life, freed from whatever bound them, becoming more fully themselves than they ever could be in flesh. And they know that one day you will wake as they woke, that you will be reunited as certainly as day follows night.

Your grief is real. But the loss is not permanent. The separation is temporary. The death that took them from you is not final. They will know you when you wake. You will know them. And what was interrupted will resume as it was, but elevated. Hold onto this. They are not gone. They are ahead of you on a path you will also walk.

FOR THE DEPRESSED

You are tired, *existentially* tired—tired of trying, tired of hoping, tired of the same challenges, tired of the monotony of daily existence. You look at your life and see no meaning, no purpose, no point to the endless cycle of waking and working and sleeping just to wake and work and sleep again. You are going through motions because stopping them seems harder than continuing them, but continuing them feels like slow suffocation.

Why are you here? Why does any of this matter? Why should you keep going when everything feels pointless, when even your best efforts produce results that barely matter and fade quickly?

Listen carefully: your depression is lying to you. Not about the pain. Not about the difficulty. But about you. About your worth. About whether anyone would notice if you disappeared.

You matter infinitely. Not because of your accomplishments or your success or your contribution. You matter because of what you *are*. Because God dwells within you. Because you are contributing to the grand inevitability of evolving deity. Because your unique perspec-

tive, your specific journey, your particular life—these are irreplaceable.

The universe needs you. Not some idealized version of you, not the
you that you wish you were. *You*, hurting, barely-holding-on you.
Because you are experiencing what needs to be experienced, learning
what needs to be learned, demonstrating what needs to be demonstrated: that beings originating from profound darkness can endure
and keep reaching for light.

You do not have to believe this truth for it to be true. You do not have
to perceive your own value for that value to be real. The depression
that tells you that you are worthless, that your life is meaningless, that
no one would miss you if you were gone—this is chemical lies, neuro-
logical malfunction, not accurate perception.

The truth is this: you are climbing. Even when it feels like falling.
Even when every day is a struggle. Even when you cannot see
progress. You are *building your soul*, and what you are building will
outlast your depression and will be yours forever.

Keep going, because the path leads somewhere real, and you are closer
to that destination than you can currently perceive.

For the Nihilistic

You have looked at the universe and concluded: there is no meaning,
no purpose, no divine plan. Just matter and energy following laws that
do not care whether you exist, that would continue exactly the same if
you had never been born.

You are sophisticated in your despair. You do not rage against mean-
inglessness—you accept it as obvious truth, as the only rational
conclusion a thinking person can reach. You smile at those who need
to believe in cosmic purpose, understanding their need but unable to
share their delusion.

But what if you are wrong? You have assumed that because the
universe does not care in the way humans care, it does not care at all.

But God is not a projection of human need. The spirit in your mind is not wish fulfillment, not a psychological crutch, not an evolved tendency toward supernatural belief. It is *real*—as real as neurons firing, as real as quantum mechanics, as real as anything that exists. It is the truest reality and purest spirit in all creation.

You dismiss experiences you cannot explain as mysteries neuroscience will eventually solve. But this is faith too—faith that materialism is sufficient, that nothing exists beyond what current science can measure, that consciousness is somehow produced by unconscious matter through processes we conveniently cannot yet describe.

What if your philosophical conclusions, however logically arrived at, are incomplete because they are based on incomplete data? What if there are realities your materialist assumptions prevent you from perceiving?

Test the alternative. Disregard blind belief and blind disbelief. Turn inward. Quiet the philosophical assumptions long enough to *listen*. See if there is something there—not supernatural, not outside nature, but deeper than you have yet perceived.

You might find that the universe is patient, not indifferent. That what looks random from a limited perspective, reveals pattern when seen from a higher vantage. That meaning is not imposed by desperate humans but sought and found by sincere ones.

Your nihilism protects you from disappointment, from false hope, from the pain of believing in things that might not be true. But it also protects you from truth itself if that truth contradicts your certainties.

Be skeptical. Be rigorous. But be *open*. You might be wrong. And if you are wrong about this, about whether existence has meaning, you are wrong about the most important thing.

The Perspective That Endures

The long view reveals that nothing which truly matters is lost. Your accomplishments on Earth? Most will be forgotten. Your reputation? Will fade. Your possessions? Will be dispersed. Your body? Will decay.

But *you*, the person you became through higher choices, the soul you constructed through values embraced and lived—this survives. This continues. This is permanent. And relationships forged in human affection? These survive too. Elevated beyond mortal limitations. But surviving, enduring, continuing without end.

And wisdom earned? This is perhaps most permanent of all. The lessons you extracted, the compassion you developed, the strength you built—this becomes everlastingly yours, contributing to who you are forever.

The universe wastes nothing. Everything worthwhile is *saved*. Preserved. Entwined into who you are becoming. The long view provides *context*—perspective that elevates how you understand what you are experiencing.

As you traverse the ascending spheres, you gain insight that transforms how you understand your own history. Problems that seemed overwhelming on lower worlds become trivial when viewed from the constellation spheres. Questions that tormented you as a mortal become almost laughably simple when you possess the knowledge and understanding you have gained.

Your trials on Earth were real. Your challenges on the mansion worlds were legitimate. But from higher vantages, you see them differently— you see how they fit into larger patterns, how they served purposes you could not perceive at the time, how they were necessary stages in becoming what you now are.

You look back at your mortal self—that confused, striving creature trying so hard to understand life with such limited tools—and you feel tenderness. You feel appreciation for the you that persisted despite having no idea what was really happening or where it would lead.

That mortal you made this possible—the you that now stands on worlds of glory, understanding truths of previously impenetrable depth, participating in realities you once had to see to believe.

Nothing was wasted. Every struggle contributed. Every painful lesson became permanent wisdom. The long view reveals that what felt like stumbling was actually climbing.

This life is not the whole story. It's just the introduction.

Why the Climb

Why all these spheres? Why this elaborate architecture of ascending worlds, this long passage from mortal death to destinations on high?

Because you cannot jump from bottom to top. You cannot leap from human mortal to perfected spirit. The distance is too great, the transformation too complete, the gap unbridgeable in a single step.

So the universe provides stairs. World after world, each a manageable step upward, each addressing specific needs, developing specific capacities, and preparing you for what comes next.

You advance at your own pace. No one rushes you. No one judges you for taking time. The universe is patient because it knows that what matters is not how quickly you move, but that you keep moving. That you keep reaching upward. That you keep allowing yourself to be refined.

And every step reveals new vistas. Every sphere shows you realities that were invisible from below. Every stage of growth brings capacities that were unattainable before.

You are becoming, realm by heavenly realm, more beautiful. More capable. More aligned with the divine nature while remaining uniquely, irreplaceably you.

This is the voyage. This is the privilege. This is the adventure that never ends, never becomes routine, never stops revealing new wonders. Keep going. The best is yet to come.

This perspective, once grasped, reaches back and transforms the present.

You find courage you didn't know you had. You can risk, can sacrifice, can give yourself fully to what matters because what you create survives your dying. The fear that held you back—fear of loss, fear of failure, fear of wasted effort—loosens its grip when you understand that nothing worthwhile is ever wasted.

Patience comes more naturally. The universe works across great timescales, and what seems like unbearable delay from mortal perspective is breathtaking speed from eternal vantage. You can endure because you know this pain is temporary, that resolution awaits.

Even difficulty carries a different weight. Challenge becomes meaningful rather than random, purposeful rather than pointless. It is material from which wisdom is extracted, experience from which character is built, temporary pain that produces undying strength.

And beneath it all, a quiet confidence takes root—not blind optimism, but grounded hope based on trajectory observed. You know where the path leads. You know that everyone who chooses so will arrive there eventually. The destination is guaranteed for all who want it.

A Letter to You

You, specifically. You reading this now, dealing with whatever troubles you, afraid of whatever you fear, grieving whatever you have lost. You are not and were never alone. The divine presence within you shares every moment of your experience. And everyone around you is in the same cosmic situation.

Your life matters more than you know. It serves purposes larger than you perceive. Your eternality is wanted by those who see what you can and will become.

Death will come. It comes for everyone. But it will not be what you fear. It will be a passage from limited to expanded, from desperation to understanding, from temporary pain to everlasting joy.

This is the long view. This is what awaits. This is why you must keep going even when going is hard. For the simple promise that you will awaken. You will be welcomed and shown everything you hoped was true…and so much more.

Keep going. Keep choosing. Keep building the soul that will wake on higher worlds. It is worth it. Every step. Every choice. All of it. Worth it.

EPILOGUE

I WROTE THIS BOOK BECAUSE I ENCOUNTERED TEACHINGS THAT changed me. Because I was shown the architecture of creation and could not keep it to myself. Because I have sat with grieving people and wished I could give them what I had found—hope grounded in something real.

This book is my attempt to share that hope. To speak to the actual pain people feel. To plainly answer the questions that burn within.

Did I succeed? That is for you to judge.

But know this: I wrote it for you. For the grieving. For the despairing. For the lost. For the seeking. For those who ache with absence and wonder if the universe cares at all.

It cares.

You will see your loved ones again—as themselves, on other and better worlds. Real places with landscaped and architecture and societies. Places where relationships continue, where growth persists, where love endures and deepens.

They woke up. They were welcomed. They are thriving.

And one day, when your time comes, when your last breath departs, you will open your new eyes and discover that the adventure has only just begun.

You will be greeted. You will be loved. You will be home.

Keep going. Keep living. Keep building the soul that will last forever.

The last rest of time has been enjoyed; the last transition sleep has been experienced; now you awake to life everlasting on the shores of the eternal abode. "And there shall be no more sleep. The presence of God and his Son are before you, and you are eternally his servants; you have seen his face, and his name is your spirit. There shall be no night there; and they need no light of the sun, for the Great Source and Center gives them light; they shall live forever and ever. And God shall wipe away all tears from their eyes; there shall be no more death, neither sorrow nor crying, neither shall there be any more pain, for the former things have passed away."[1]

FROM THE AUTHOR

Thank you for reading. This book is the culmination of twenty years of spiritual seeking, study, and reflection.

If you're willing to share your thoughts, reader reviews make a meaningful difference for independent authors. Thank you so much.

APPENDIX

The information in this book is drawn from *The Urantia Book*, a 2,097 page book first published in 1955 that claims to be a revelation presented by celestial beings to clarify and expand human understanding of cosmic reality and our place within it. This book about angels exclusively cites the 1955 edition which is in the public domain.

You may have never heard of it. Or you may have heard of it and dismissed it. That's fine. What matters is whether the information resonates as true, whether it elevates your understanding, whether it helps you live with greater purpose and confidence.

The Urantia Book has its critics and its devoted students. It's been called everything from the most important spiritual text of the modern era to elaborate fiction. I'm not asking you to accept it blindly. I'm asking you to read it and *then* decide if you think it is true. I do, and I have read it countless times.

The source is less important than the truth it contains. And if you want to explore further, *The Urantia Book* is available online and in print.

ABOUT THE SOURCE MATERIAL

The Urantia Book is a comprehensive revelatory tome covering a wide variety of subjects including cosmology, philosophy, history and spirituality. It describes the nature of reality from the perspective of celestial beings and provides detailed information about the structure of the universe, the nature of God, the purpose of human existence, and the journey of the soul after death.

The book is organized into 196 papers grouped into four parts:

Part I: The Central and Superuniverses

Part II: The Local Universe

Part III: The History of Urantia (Earth)

Part IV: The Life and Teachings of Jesus

This book, *Where We Go When We Die*, draws from Parts I, II, and III.

While I do, at times, exercise creative license, my intention is never to stray from what the book discloses as revelatory fact. Any mistakes are mine to own and correct.

Italicized passages throughout this book are drawn from The Urantia Book, either verbatim or closely paraphrased. Many have been slightly condensed, combined, edited, or adapted for brevity and narrative continuity while preserving the essential meaning and terminology of the original text.

The following references are organized by chapter to help readers locate the source material corresponding to specific content in this book.

NOTES

INTRODUCTION

1. Paper 102, Introduction: The Foundations of Religious Faith

1. THE LAST BREATH AND THE FIRST AWAKENING

1. Paper 112, Section 5: Personality Survival, Survival of the Human Self
2. Paper 47, Section 3: The Seven Mansion Worlds, The First Mansion World
3. Paper 112, Section 5: Personality Survival, Survival of the Human Self

2. THE MANSION WORLDS

1. Paper 47, Introduction: The Seven Mansion Worlds
2. Paper 47, Section 4: The Seven Mansion Worlds, The Second Mansion World
3. Paper 47, Section 3: The Seven Mansion Worlds, The First Mansion World
4. Paper 47, Section 3: The Seven Mansion Worlds, The First Mansion World
5. Paper 47, Section 6: The Seven Mansion Worlds, The Fourth Mansion World
6. Paper 47, Section 7: The Seven Mansion Worlds, The Fifth Mansion World
7. Paper 47, Section 8: The Seven Mansion Worlds, The Sixth Mansion World
8. Paper 47, Section 8: The Seven Mansion Worlds, The Sixth Mansion World
9. Paper 47, Section 9: The Seven Mansion Worlds, The Seventh Mansion World

3. REUNION

1. Foreward, Section V: Personality Realities
2. Paper 28, Section 5: Ministering Spirits of the Superuniverses, The Tertiary Seconaphim

4. THE SYSTEM HEADQUARTERS

1. Paper 47, Section 10: The Seven Mansion Worlds, Jerusem Citizenship
2. Paper 46, Section 2: The Local System Headquarters, Physical Features of Jerusem
3. Paper 46, Section 4: The Local System Headquarters, Residential and Administrative Areas
4. Paper 46, Section 4: The Local System Headquarters, Residential and Administrative Areas
5. Paper 46, Section 5: The Local System Headquarters, The Jerusem Circles
6. Paper 45, Section 1: The Local System Administration, Transitional Culture Worlds

5. THE CONSTELLATION WORLDS

6. THE LOCAL UNIVERSE

7. THE SUPERUNIVERSE

8. HAVONA

1. Paper 14, Introduction: The Central and Divine Universe
2. Paper 14, Section 5: The Central and Divine Universe, Life in Havona
3. Paper 14, Section 5: The Central and Divine Universe, Life in Havona
4. Paper 14, Section 5: The Central and Divine Universe, Life in Havona
5. Paper 2, Section 7: The Nature of God, The Divine Character
6. Paper 56, Section 10: Universal Unity, Truth, Beauty, and Goodness
7. Paper 19, Section 6: The Co-ordinate Trinity-Origin Beings, Havona Natives
8. Paper 14, Section 4: The Central and Divine Universe, Creatures of the Central Universe
9. Paper 19, Section 6: The Co-ordinate Trinity-Origin Beings, Havona Natives
10. Paper 6, Section 4: The Eternal Son, Attributes of the Eternal Son

9. PARADISE

1. Paper 11, Section 1: The Eternal Isle of Paradise, The Divine Residence
2. Paper 11, Introduction: The Eternal Isle of Paradise
3. Paper 11, Section 5: The Eternal Isle of Paradise, Nether Paradise
4. Paper 11, Section 1: The Eternal Isle of Paradise, The Divine Residence
5. Paper 31, Section 3: The Corps of the Finality, Glorified Mortals
6. Paper 31, Section 3: The Corps of the Finality, Glorified Mortals
7. Paper 31, Section 3: The Corps of the Finality, Glorified Mortals
8. Paper 48, Section 8: The Morontia Life, The Morontia Progressors
9. Paper 11, Section 9: The Eternal Isle of Paradise, The Uniqueness of Paradise
10. Paper 27, Section 1: Ministry of the Primary Supernaphim, Instigators of Rest

10. THE GODS OF PARADISE

1. Paper 8, Section 3: The Infinite Spirit, The Third Source and Center
2. Paper 9, Section 8: Relation of the Infinite Spirit to the Universe, The Spirit of Personal Ministry
3. Paper 8, Section 1: The Infinite Spirit, The God of Action
4. Paper 8, Section 2: The Infinite Spirit, Nature of the Infinite Spirit
5. Paper 8, Section 6: The Infinite Spirit, Personality of the Infinite Spirit
6. Paper 8, Section 6: The Infinite Spirit, Personality of the Infinite Spirit
7. Paper 9, Section 5: Relation of the Infinite Spirit to the Universe, The Mind Ministry
8. Paper 8, Section 4: The Infinite Spirit, The Divine Spirit
9. Paper 8, Section 4: The Infinite Spirit, The Divine Spirit
10. Paper 7, Section 1: Relation of the Eternal Son to the Universe, Spirit-Gravity Circuit
11. Paper 7, Section 3: Relation of the Eternal Son to the Universe, Relation of the Eternal Son to the Individual
12. Paper 7, Section 3: Relation of the Eternal Son to the Universe, Relation of the Eternal Son to the Individual
13. Paper 6, Introduction: The Eternal Son

11. THE DIVINE GIFT

12. SURVIVAL

13. THE RELIGION OF EXPERIENCE

14. THE PURPOSE OF AFFLICTION

15. PERFECTION THROUGH IMPERFECTION

16. THE SUPREME

6. Paper 101, Section 6: The Real Nature of Religion, Progressive Religious Experience
7. Paper 26, Section 6: Ministering Spirits of the Central Universe, The Supremacy Guides
8. Paper 117, Section 4: God the Supreme, The Finite God
9. Paper 117, Section 6: God the Supreme, The Quest for the Supreme

17. THE EVOLUTION OF EVERYTHING

1. Paper 12, Introduction: The Universe of Universes
2. Paper 65, Section 6: The Overcontrol of Evolution, Evolutionary Techniques of Life
3. Paper 12, Section 1: The Universe of Universes, Space Levels of the Master Universe
4. Paper 12, Section 2: The Universe of Universes, The Domains of the Unqualified Absolute
5. Paper 12, Section 2: The Universe of Universes, The Domains of the Unqualified Absolute
6. Paper 65, Section 4: The Overcontrol of Evolution, The Urantia Adventure
7. Paper 65, Section 4: The Overcontrol of Evolution, The Urantia Adventure
8. Paper 65, Section 1: The Overcontrol of Evolution, Life Carrier Functions
9. Paper 65, Section 8: The Overcontrol of Evolution, Evolution in Time and Space
10. Paper 12, Section 6: The Universe of Universes, Universal Overcontrol
11. Paper 65, Section 8: The Overcontrol of Evolution, Evolution in Time and Space

18. THE CRAFT OF BECOMING

1. Paper 44, Section 7: The Celestial Artisans, The Harmony Workers
2. Paper 132, Section 2: The Discourse on Truth and Beauty, Good and Evil
3. Paper 111, Section 4: The Adjuster and the Soul, The Inner Life
4. Paper 44, Section 8: The Celestial Artisans, Mortal Aspirations and Morontia Achievements

EPILOGUE

1. Paper 27, Section 1: Ministry of the Primary Supernaphim, Instigators of Rest

ABOUT THE AUTHOR

Michael Vincent spent years searching for answers that religion couldn't provide. Then he discovered *The Urantia Book*—a dense revelation that answered his questions with a coherence he'd never encountered.

His work translates this complex material into books anyone can absorb. Not spiritual platitudes—specific, detailed information about how reality actually works.

Where We Go When We Die is part of that project. Other books cover angels, cosmic history, Jesus, human origins, and the structure of the universe itself.

michaelvincentauthor.com

instagram.com/michaelvincent_author
tiktok.com/@michael.vincent.author
youtube.com/@MichaelVincent-Author
amazon.com/author/havona-press

ALSO BY MICHAEL VINCENT

The Missing Years: The Real Story of Jesus Beyond the Gospels (The *Universe Maker from Nazareth* series, Book One)

Fusion with God: The Path to Immortality

The Angelic Orders: Cosmic Servants of the Infinite

Upcoming Books:

The Public Ministry: The Real Story of Jesus Beyond the Gospels (The *Universe Maker from Nazareth* series, Book Two)

The Final Week: The Real Story of Jesus Beyond the Gospels (The *Universe Maker from Nazareth* series, Book Three)

The Nine Races: The Forgotten Origin of Humanity

Before Humans: The Drama of World-Making

Marcus Aurelius, Rodan of Alexandria, and Jesus of Nazareth: A Philosopher's Journey